JIMMY CARTER
and
AMERICAN FANTASY
PSYCHOHISTORICAL EXPLORATIONS

Edited by

Lloyd deMause and Henry Ebel

Two Continents/Psychohistory Press

Library of Congress Cataloging in Publication Data

Main entry under title:

Jimmy Carter and American fantasy.

   Includes index.
   1. Carter, Jimmy, 1924—   —Addresses, essays, lectures. 2. Presidents—United
States—Biography—Addresses, essays, lectures. 3. Carter, Jimmy, 1924—   —
Personality—Addresses, essays, lectures. I. deMause, Lloyd. II. Ebel, Henry, 1938-
E873.J55   973.926'092'4   [B]   77-9146
ISBN 0-8467-9363-7

"A collective mental process is hard to conceive of, but that is not my fault. So is the individual mind as it is known from psychoanalysis hard to conceive of. . ."

—Rudolph Binion

Published in conjunction with
THE INSTITUTE FOR PSYCHOHISTORY

For a list of other publications of The Institute and its Psychohistory Press, write: The Institute for Psychohistory, 2315 Broadway, New York, New York 10024 (212) 873-3331.

CONTENTS

EDITORS' FOREWORD

Psychohistory as a profession is now barely five years old. Although psychoanalytic studies of history began with Freud, and although our *Bibliography of Psychohistory* lists almost a thousand items, the actual birth of psychohistory as an independent discipline belongs only to the 1970s, when we started our first professional journal, our first separate institutes, and our first international association. The number of college courses given in psychohistory has jumped from two to over two hundred in the four years since we began *The Journal of Psychohistory,* and important psychohistorical works are now appearing regularly, attracting widespread—if often violently hostile—attention from the general public. For better or for worse, psychohistory as an independent discipline has begun in earnest.

The popular image of psychohistory, however—as a club with which to hit the unsuspecting famous over the head—has nothing to do with what modern psychohistory is about. First of all, although childhood continues to be one main focus of our studies, our professional training demands we achieve an empathy with those we study which precludes the kind of simplistic psychiatric labeling that has often been the style of past studies. Secondly, our studies more and more concentrate on *group,* not individual, psychohistory, focusing on *shared* psychological patterns—a focus which considers the old-fashioned psychobiographical approach as too limited to explain real history.

That our new science of psychohistory is radically innovative, and challenges old ideas of political history, we readily admit. That it is anchored in a growing body of empirical evidence, however, is our only claim to respect. That these psychohistorical explorations will be fruitful—not only in new insights, but also in helping to avoid the very disasters we ourselves have predicted—is our fervent hope, one which we know every reader will share.

Lloyd deMause
Henry Ebel

CHAPTER ONE

Jimmy Carter and American Fantasy

LLOYD
DE MAUSE

It has been four and a half years since America has been at war. This is a long time for peace to last—at least if recent experience is any guide, and if near-wars like the Cuban Missile Crisis are counted. The first question, therefore, that one should ask of a new President is obviously: "Will he take us into war?"

The results of this study give a simple, if frightening, answer to this question. Our conclusion is that Jimmy Carter—for reasons rooted both in his own personality and in the powerful emotional demands of American fantasy—is very likely to lead us into a new war by 1979.

Which crisis might be chosen to act out our fantasy needs is not our concern here, since our focus is wholly American. Nor can we give an exact timetable or scenario for the next crisis. Even so, and with all due respect to the tentativeness of predictions made in our young science of psychohistory, we must conclude that it appears that Jimmy Carter is very likely to be our next war leader not too far in the future.

That no one usually considers this blunt but crucial question—whether a leader might take us to war—is due more to our fear of hearing the answer than to any inherent difficulties in asking the question. After all, modern depth psychology is now able to determine emotional maturity of personality in at least some rough sense and feel reasonably certain of its findings. Modern psychohistory is also, by now, able to determine the general emotional mood of a nation—again, with some rough degree of accuracy—and show how our shifting national emotional needs interact with our leader's personality to produce moments of national crisis.[1]

But psychohistory to date has mainly been written about the distant past—the more distant, the better. Since we are *part* of the group-fantasies of today, how can we possibly analyze them? The five studies in this volume begin this most difficult task. They are a first try at measuring the emotional maturity of a current President, Jimmy Carter, relating his personality to the emotional needs of the American people, and predicting what the immediate future is likely to bring as a result of the interaction between the two.

THE ORIGIN OF THIS STUDY

This study of Jimmy Carter and American fantasy is the fifth of some twenty-two projects currently being sponsored by The Institute for Psychohistory, its *Journal of Psychohistory,* and The Psychohistory Press.[2] The project began in the summer of 1976 at the regular Summer Workshop of the Institute, where several Research Associates began preliminary discussions of Paul Elovitz's initial report on Carter's childhood and personality—particularly in relation to the kinds of unconscious fantasies the media were at that time creating around him, from his teeth imagery to his various messianic "outsider" roles. Over the past year, our research and discussions have continued at Institute meetings and in private smaller gatherings, so that, as in all our Institute projects, it soon became hard to tell whose ideas were whose, so free-flowing and "non-academic" were our discussions and our sharing of individual research results. Even so, we have ended up writing from five quite different perspectives and have focused on five different areas of personal interest.

My own research has been concentrated on repeated patterns of American group-fantasy over the past quarter century of American politics. Paul Elovitz's interest has sent him to Plains, Georgia, for psychoanalytically-informed interviews with Lillian Carter and other emotionally crucial figures in Jimmy Carter's early life. David Beisel has tried to be more synthetic in approach than any of us, focusing on the complex interaction between personality traits and American historical fantasy needs. John Hartman has focused on utopian group-fantasies surrounding Carter's nominating Convention, and Henry Ebel has given us an inner glimpse of the way we all unconsciously perceive our leaders as super-potent adults and as super-babies at the same time. Yet all of the studies converge on one central theme: the intimate, dynamic relation-ship between the unconscious needs of the leader and the equally deep unconscious needs of the group he purports to "lead."

Since psychohistory, as we conceive of it at the Institute for Psychohistory, strives to be a science of patterns of historical motivation, our discussions and subsequent research have focused primarily on two areas crucial to the analysis of Jimmy Carter's motivational dynamics. The first is his childhood—what did it *feel* like to be the son of Lillian and James Earl Carter, in the late 1920's, in Plains, Georgia? What strengths and what weaknesses did Carter acquire during his formative years from his relationship with his parents and other caretakers? What personality traits, what general patterns of behavior, have remained dominant throughout his life to determine the way he reacts to the enormous emotional tasks put on him as our leader?

The second main focus of study is that of historical "group-fantasy," a term which I use psychohistorically in a rather more specific way than it is used in the field of small-group dynamics, from which I borrowed it. An historical group-fantasy is a set of shared unconscious assumptions, quite unrelated to any "objective" reality, about the way it *feels* to be a member of a historical group at a particular time in history. Group-fantasies are what national opinion polls attempt to capture when they periodically try to determine the "mood" of America, and ask people whether they feel their leader is strong or weakening, whether they feel the country is safe or in a state of turmoil, whether the enemy is strong or threatening, what they feel the future may bring, and so on. These "gut" feeling change in patterns which, in fact, have nothing to do with the actual condition of the country. As we will shortly discover, they are almost wholly due to shifting fantasies constructed by people, and communicated by the media, which center on the leader's ability to provide imaginary nurturance to the "led." But these shifts in "mood" are nevertheless real, they can be measured, they move in roughly predictable ways, *and* they determine when we choose to participate in or abstain from international conflict.

One final word on the Carter project before I begin the presentation of my evidence. The demands of group-fantasy in America today are such that the majority of the press, including reviewers, will probably refer to these essays as an "attack" on Jimmy Carter. Nothing could be further from the truth. Indeed, quite the opposite. I even suspect that Carter would both enjoy and profit from reading these studies. In point of fact, we all voted for him, but even if we hadn't, our empathy—which is the first condition of our task as professional psychohistorians—has allowed us over the past year of research to so continuously identify with him, both as a growing child and as an adult, that by now he seems like one of us, a friend, hardly someone we could unfeelingly "attack." Besides, he is *our* leader—*we* are the passengers on the ship he is piloting through international waters, and we would ourselves be participating in the common group-fantasy that no one really dies in wars if we wished him anything but well. Let it be said at the outset: Jimmy Carter is a decent, personally attractive, well-intentioned human being. But matters of war and peace involve the very deepest layers of the personality, and it is unfortunately likely that if the day should come when we are all evaporated by that bright orange glow on the horizon, it will be a decent, well-intentioned man who will have pushed the button.

STAGES OF AMERICAN GROUP-FANTASY

The political roles each of us plays within the shifting group-fantasies of our national life are, of course, roles both derived from and acting as defenses against childhood anxieties.[3] But even though one person may tend to take on liberal roles and another conservative ones, depending on the respective amounts of strictness and support in childhood, there is a higher fantasy level which views these roles as merely two parts played in a drama that encompasses both, one whose "script" transcends the usual left-right political dichotomy of modern politics. Thus, America may split on temporary issues, but as a rule the vast majority of the country unites on major political assumptions: we unite in wanting our leader and nation "strong," we unite in feeling that the leader is often too strong and the government too big, we unite in agreeing to split over minor matters so as to make certain that no substantial changes can take place, we unite on who the "enemy" is and how dangerous he is, we unite on when it is time to go to war, and when it is time to end a war.

It is this higher level of group-fantasy which I have attempted in recent years to conceptualize and then measure. The tool for this measurement I have termed "Fantasy Analysis." The detailed technical criteria for the Fantasy Analysis of any historical document will be found in another of my essays,[4] but suffice to to say here that it involves extracting from the historical document all the operative fantasy terms, including all the metaphors, similes, feeling states, body images, and other key emotional terms present. This produces a series of words describing deep body feelings, which then can be analyzed and placed in psychohistorical perspective.

As just one example out of hundreds I elsewhere detail, here is a passage from the minutes of a Senate Foreign Relations Committee Hearing in 1949 discussing our posture vis-à-vis the Russians in Germany:[5]

We understand that there are powerful pulls in the other direction and that there are things which the Russians would do which would be important in any such situation as that. We have no doubt that

at some time or other the Russians are going to get ready to sell the
Poles down the river on the eastern boundary.

A Fantasy Analysis of this passage would pick up only two terms:
"pulls . . . down the river." (Generally a Fantasy Analysis condenses
documents to about 1% of their total verbiage.) The rest of the words are
considered non-operative in motivational terms, essentially defensive in
purpose, "rational" covers serving to distract one's attention from the
emotionally powerful fantasy language buried within.

Now this may appear at first sight thoroughly arbitrary, and I admit
that with any less than 50 pages of illustration and discussion it will be
difficult for me to convey the accuracy and trustworthiness of this new
psychohistorical tool. But even in the case of this 1949 hearing, it turns
out that the words "pulls . . . down the river" sound the emotional
theme of the whole meeting, and condense very well its main historical
group-fantasy: that the group's actions in taking a harder line against the
Russians on Germany may result in its being pulled down a dangerous,
"squeezing" passageway against its wishes, and that something
terrifying might happen. Thus, although the full text of the Hearing
reads in a rather controlled and even dull tone, the Fantasy Analysis of
the opening sections reads as follows:

> hurting . . . face saver . . . riposte . . . large voice . . . horse's
> mouth . . . lay down . . . undermine . . . pussyfoot . . . terrified
> . . .terror . . . terror . . . pull . . . pulled . . . pulls . . . down the
> river . . . forced . . . driven . . . afraid . . . pull . . . run out . . .
> down the river . . . war . . . pull . . . fear . . . break . . . insane . . .
> squeezed . . . corridor . . . corridor . . . corridor . . . corridor . . .

What I found from performing Fantasy Analyses of hundreds of
historical documents—including newspaper and magazine articles,
committee hearings, speeches, press conferences, political cartoons,
even the Nixon Watergate tapes—is that hidden within every group
communication is the skeleton of an emotionally powerful set of body
feelings, and that a large part of the time this message has to do with
body memories stemming from the primary trauma of all our lives: birth.

Although this discovery of birth as the key to group-fantasy appears at
first to be a rather astonishing and even bizarre finding, it is the outcome
of several years of analytic effort, and was in fact produced "by the
material" rather than being imposed upon it for any theoretical reasons.
(Indeed, I was so thoroughly disbelieving for some time of the nature of
the results, that I retested the Fantasy Analysis technique with people
unfamiliar with my earlier work to be certain I wasn't reading into the
material something that wasn't there.) The selection above is one typical

version or stage of this body memory, one which regularly occurs as the result of Fantasy Analyses of historical material. It depicts a moment prior to the onset of actual birth, when the fetus is just beginning to feel the pull "down the river" and "into the corridor," when the "squeeze" of the mother's contractions is just beginning to produce "terror" of what lies ahead—the seemingly endless hours of enormous persecutory pressure of the birth itself.

Since I am unable to go into as much detail here about the way birth stages affect group-fantasies as I have done in other studies,[6] I can only say in summary that the results of my Fantasy Analysis of hundreds of public documents from recent American history show a regular, lawful pattern of stages of group-fantasy, a pattern which repeats itself over and over again every three or four years, as follows:

ILLUSTRATION 1

STAGES OF GROUP-FANTASY

Fetal Stage	Leader Fantasy	Nation (womb) Fantasy	Enemy Fantasy
FS1 "Strong"	Leader Strong	Intact womb, safe inside	Enemy strong, at bay
FS2 "Cracking"	Weakening	Cracking, crowded, unsafe	Weakening. dangerous
FS3 "Collapse"	Helpless	Collapsed, pressures building	Collapsed, poisonous
FS4 "Upheaval"	Tough	Trapped, fight way out of choking womb	Enemy powerful, engaged

The conditions within each stage were consistently correlated in historical documents subjected to Fantasy Analysis. In stage one, when the leader is strong—often but not always at the beginning of a presidential term—the nation seems safe and the "enemy" is kept at bay. Politics seems to be centered around the personality of a nurturant fantasy-leader, and to consist of discussions of how strong he is, whether he is *too* strong, whether government is doing enough, or is too big, and so on. In time, the ability of the leader to sustain a role of total magical nurturance to his people begins to deteriorate, and the "Cracking" stage two begins. News articles proliferate on how the internal strains in our country are threatening our national strength, on how a sudden collapse of values is to be feared, and on how the enemy too (projectively) seems to be "cracking at the seams," with crises of leadership that may make them unstable and therefore dangerous. Stage three, "Collapse," often begins with a specific event that can be viewed as a "collapse of values" which the fantasy-leader is helpless to prevent—whether a set of local events, such as riots, or an external event, such as a foreign policy reverse. During this stage, the central focus of anxiety is: Can the helpless leader protect us against possible upheavals and catastrophes? Articles are written on how crowded the world (or the cities or the highways) is getting, how slender the food supply is, how polluted the environment has become, and how sheer chaos is just around the corner. Finally, with stage four, "Upheaval," birth itself begins, and the nation looks for some crisis, usually involving war or the threat of war, to get into. The nation feels trapped, choking, claustrophobic, and must engage in a "struggle for freedom" in order to fight its way out of an intolerable situation. After a crisis situation is located, the enemy is engaged, and the nation feels strong again—and also greatly relieved, because at least it is now actively fighting something in the real world rather than passively suffering the fantasied intolerable pressures. (Political cartoons of the head hurting from painful pressures, and of the body being stretched and twisted, mark this stage.) But if the leader cannot "win" the war within a year or so, the nation fears it is not so tough after all and may actually die during its birth-crisis, and the leader is then instructed by the fantasy-language of all the media at once that somehow the birth pains must be ended. The leader then ends the war (at least in fantasy), the leader is once again strong, and the cycle repeats itself all over again.

The actual evidence for this group-fantasy cycle is detailed, document by document, in my study "The Fetal Origins of History," with Fantasy Analyses of the media, speeches, conferences, congressional hearings, tapes, political cartoons and other material for the past 25 years of American history. The results of this analysis have been summarized in Chart A.

The past 25 years of American history have seen 6 complete group-fantasy cycles, each birth stage finally being acted out in a real crisis, generally, though not always, in a war or a near-war. The captions above the line show the crisis which was chosen to act out the birth fantasy at the peak of each cycle. The international crisis has usually been provided by whatever was handy at the time, and in every case *the fantasy preceded the reality.* That is, the fantasy language first went up to stage four, and the nation was crying for relief from intolerable pressures, and *then* whatever crisis was around was deemed important enough to produce action on our part. To emphasize this point, I have also put *below* the line some of the international crises which occurred during the first three stages, just a few of many that actually occurred, to show how many crises we did *not* choose to get into. Most of these, like the fall of the French forces in Indo-China, the Suez invasion, and various Arab-Israeli wars, were just as "important," often even more so, than the events we chose to jump into, but we were not under sufficient psychological pressure to respond with war-like action until we reached the fourth or "Upheaval" stage.

The first fantasy cycle begins with the slow buildup in the early Eisenhower years. It helps explain why Eisenhower could, during stage three, coolly withstand the powerful forces trying to get us to send planes and even troops into Dienbienphu, but then a little while later, at stage four, suddenly alert the nation and ask for formal war powers from Congress over a few insignificant islands off Formosa. Eisenhower's second cycle has a similar pattern, first careful restraint (during stage two) and refusal to commit our troops in the Suez-crisis, followed unexpectedly, and almost without rhyme or reason, by the dispatch of U.S. troops to peaceful Lebanon when we again reached stage four and couldn't find any other crisis to become involved in.

Kennedy's single cycle reached the fourth level early in 1961, and although for a time it looked as if we would be able to act it out in an armed confrontation with the Russians over Berlin, they seemed reluctant (for their own reasons) to get into a fight at that time, and built the Berlin Wall instead, thus ending the "crisis"—but leaving America "hanging" in mid-air at the "Upheaval" level. As we moved into 1962, we were therefore badly in need of something to fight about, but with no active war around to get into, the media began to comment on the "strange calm" the world seemed to be afflicted by—there was such cognitive dissonance between the upheaval and terror of the group-fantasy in our heads and the "quiet" of the world outside that we thought we might be insane. By the summer of 1962, we found the solution: Cuba. Long before we even suspected there might be missiles there, we began to use war-like language against Cuba, passing war resolutions, calling Cuba a "cancer" on America, declaring a blockade of the island, terming Castro's existence and a "Red Cuba" intolerable to us, and then sending U-2 planes over to see what we could discover. The actual finding of the missiles after all this fantasy came as a great emotional relief, and when the Russians agreed to remove them in exchange for what we admitted were totally useless missiles in Turkey, which we had decided to remove anyway, we turned down the offer, gave the order to invade the island, and risked starting World War III—all so we could actually engage or at least thoroughly humiliate the poisonous "enemy" and experience the catharsis of fantasied birth.

Johnson's crisis was of course the Vietnam war, and although we may have "inched" our way into it, the fact is that our first actual combat troops were sent to Vietnam only a week after the group-fantasy language reached stage four in every periodical in the country. Yet Vietnam, like both world wars before it, was a very unsatisfactory catharsis—it didn't seem to want to follow its fantasy script and to end when we "felt" it should. So after months of articles and protests in 1968, demonstrating how many of "our boys" were dying there (at the fantasy level, no one seems to die early on in a war), Johnson "ended the war" by announcing its de-escalation and his own retirement. Immediately, two things happened to the group-fantasy. First, fantasy language went right back to stage one, and the war virtually disappeared from the media. It was as though, by common consent, we had agreed to pretend that it was over, though of course in fact it was still escalating, and the biggest battles and most destructive bombings lay in the future. Those who still protested, the same protesters that earlier captured fond media attention, were now vilified as nuts and crazies—why protest when the war had ended?

Nixon was elected, and went through the usual cycle of strong and then weakening leadership, and when at length in 1970 we got back up to stage four again, we began looking around for a new crisis in which to act out our birth fantasies. We looked at the world situation and discovered—lo and behold—Vietnam! Three weeks after the group-fantasy language again reached stage four, Nixon ordered the invasion of Cambodia, and the media quite rightly declared that "a new war" had begun.

By 1971, this "new war" again began to be painful enough to end, and the U.S. Senate did what it could easily have done years earlier; it voted to terminate the war. The fantasy language immediately dropped back to stage one again (although, as with Korea before it, the war actually dragged on for another year and a half after our fantasy declared it had ended). Nixon got the peace message from the nation and announced his purely symbolic trip to China—since he was now a "strong" leader again and could easily bargain with "the enemy."

But by the time the sixth cycle on our chart again reached stage four, Nixon found he had no crisis anywhere around to get into; indeed, he was just in the process of *actually* ending the Vietnam war. The Middle East was once again very tempting, but just managed to evade becoming a real crisis. Therefore, Nixon made the ultimate sacrifice—if the weak leader can't prevent the crisis, he will *become* the crisis, and by removing himself give a new leader a chance to go through the strong-weakening-helpless-tough cycle. Watergate, which previously had been buried in the back pages, now moved to the "front burner" of national attention, and Nixon, trained in self-sacrifice from birth, threw *himself* into the flames "to relieve the intolerable pressures." Here the Watergate tapes

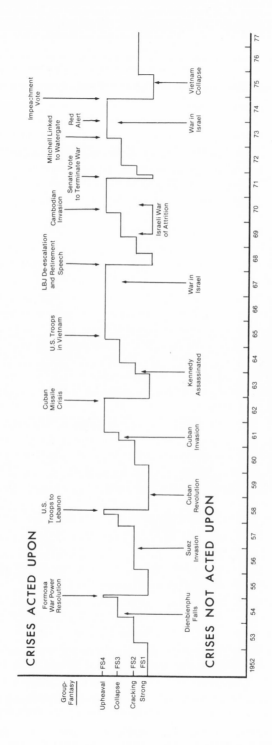

CHART A — LEVELS OF AMERICAN GROUP-FANTASY

are invaluable evidence of the movement of group-fantasy over the months, and a long analysis of the tapes and other documents from the Watergate "crisis" are part of my "Fetal Origins of History" article, along with a discussion of the special conditions under which a nation can substitute the replacement of a leader for the catharsis of war. But even during the Watergate period, the fourth stage crisis in 1973 *did* involve a plunge into a near-war action. After the last Arab-Israeli war had ended, Nixon ordered a full "Red Alert," and two million American troops prepared for war, including the arming of nuclear weapons—all over a thoroughly insignificant Russian message about U.N. peace-keeping forces.[7] The Russians didn't respond, of course, so the crisis was kept at a fantasy level until the impeachment vote finally removed the weak leader.

After Nixon's removal, Ford became our stage one leader, and was everywhere shown as strong and nurturant, at least until he had been in office for some time and was shot at by two different women. He then appeared weak and ineffectual (stage two), a joke to many. When Jimmy Carter became President, because of the length of time since the last crisis, he started out at stage two in group-fantasy—which explains why he has barely had any "honeymoon" period in which he could get programs through Congress, as has been common with the beginning of other presidencies. Carter's Gallup Poll after four months in office shows only 66% of those polled approving of the way he does his job, compared to 82% for Truman, 74% for Eisenhower, 76% for Kennedy and 73% for Johnson after a similar period.[8] This "lack of strength" image is wholly due to the stage of group-fantasy we are in at the time of this writing (May, 1977), which calls for a weakening (stage two) leader. In *reality* terms, Carter became President at the best of times—a sharply rising economy, no war, no civil strife—and no President has worked harder to strengthen his image with the people during his first months. But in *group-fantasy* terms, he remains a weakening leader, certain to weaken even further during the coming year. This is why his bills are already running into trouble, even though they have been rather modest in scope compared to the early proposals of other Presidents, and this is also why those polled continue to complain that in some indefinable way they still haven't been able to "really know" what he is like.

THE PRESIDENT AS FANTASY LEADER

It should be understood at the outset that any actual accomplishments of a nation and its leadership are achieved *despite* the process of group-fantasy—fantasy works to defeat all real accomplishments, to handcuff all real leadership qualities, to waste all real assets and to keep people wholly passive. Even wars turn out to be passive group acts—no decisions are required that are not purely tactical, no painful compromises of values, no maturity, only pure emotional release. America was never so passive and uncreative as in the Vietnam years (Vietnam indeed killed The Great Society, as Johnson said it did, only far more profoundly than just economically). In fact, I have elsewhere presented evidence that the President, his advisors, the Congress and most of the people in the nation enter into what is an actual *trance state* while communicating and acting out these group-fantasies, a genuine trance similar to that of hypnotism or to that experienced under certain drugs. A group of presidential advisors sitting around a table in a War Room (as in the Cuban Missile Crisis) or a group of Congressmen attending hearings on war-powers legislation (as in the Gulf of Tonkin Crisis) are participating in what is technically more like a séance than a rational discussion. Their trance-like state can even be documented (with some effort—verbatim minutes are rarely kept of actual decision-making meetings, and memories of what really happened are notoriously skimpy). All the elements of a trance state can nevertheless be seen in these meetings: heightened suggestibility, increased dependence on the leader, extremes of passivity by usually forceful people, demands for group unanimity, emotional rather than logical thinking, amnesia for inconvenient facts, inability to tolerate inaction, and even an increase in such body feelings as dizziness, fears of loss of control, dry mouth, pressures in the head, increased heart rate and feelings of claustrophobia, all of which are related to birth memories.[10]

The notion of the President as primarily a fantasy leader who is a delegate of national moods is quite at odds with the traditional model of political science, which regards leaders primarily as holders of something called "power" which they use to get action. In fact, most of politics works in an exactly opposite fashion: the nation first develops quite irrational group-fantasies, then pumps them through the media and lower government officials into the President and his advisors, expecting them to somehow act them out in order to relieve the anxieties generated by the fantasied conditions. This is true regardless of nation, period, or form of government. I have elsewhere documented the presence, for instance, of powerful birth emotions of being choked, trapped and strangled in the words of many nations going to war, from Kaiser Wilhelm's declaration before World War I that he felt "strangled" because a "net had suddenly been thrown over our head" to Hitler's going to war to solve Germany's problem of "Lebensraum." Similarly, America's wars from the Revolution to Vietnam have been permeated by language like "the child Independence struggling for birth," "a descent into the abyss," and the inability "to see the light at the end of the tunnel."[12] Although geopolitical or economic motives are usually presumed to be the cause of wars, they are more accurately the *occasions* for war, the real causes being psychodynamic, wholly internal and shared psychological states. When the German General Staff wrote in 1914 that they "took to extreme measures in order to burn out with a glowing iron the cancer that has constantly threatened to poison the body of Europe," they used the same language and were responding to the same fantasy as Richard Nixon when, before the Cuban Missile Crisis, he said that "Cuba is a cancer . . . war is risked if Communism is not stopped and is allowed to spread now."[13]

The responsibility for solving this fantasy is finally dumped into the lap of the fantasy leader, who is an expert at receiving and interpreting the inchoate, powerful, shifting fantasy needs of large groups of people (this being the very definition of a politician). The "pressures" of the moment are translated into action-solutions and the fears of the people become the commands of the leader. The enormous relief provided by violent action is shown in Churchill's letter to his wife in 1914, as Europe went to war: "Everything tends toward catastrophe and collapse. I am interested, geared up and happy." A similar group mood is revealed in what one American wrote from Washington, D.C. on the day Truman decided to send U.S. troops to Korea:

> I have lived and worked in and out of this city for twenty years. Never before . . . have I felt such a sense of relief and unity pass through this city . . . When the President's statement was read in the House, the entire chamber rose to cheer.[14]

Perhaps one of my most surprising findings has been that the frequency and seriousness of wars and war-like actions has little to do with the realities of military force, realities which supposedly govern so much of international relations. For instance, Truman's presidency was conducted in a continuous state of panic, culminating in his plunging America into the bloody, protracted Korean war—all during a period when America had overwhelming superiority of all forces, including sole delivery capacity for the atomic bomb. Indeed, the Truman Doctrine, the basis for a quarter-century of world-wide American intervention in local politics, was proclaimed in 1947 at a time when America enjoyed an atomic monopoly and when Russia lay utterly prostrate from World War II damage to her industry and population, a moment which Dean Acheson described as one of the greatest crises in history, when Russia was about to "carry infection to Africa through Asia Minor and Egypt, and to Europe through Italy and France."[15] In contrast, Eisenhower's years were far less interventionist, and were wholly without actual war, despite America's loss of military preponderance after Russian nuclear and missile development. It is, in fact, solely our fantasy needs which

prevent us from seeing that internal dynamics, not external threats, govern
our foreign policy.

Actual shooting wars, then, begin when two nations, in a slow, deadly
dance, match group-fantasy cycles, wave for wave, crest for crest, and
agree to grapple through a birth together—agreeing, as Khrushchev wrote
to Kennedy at the height of the Cuban Missile Crisis, to "come to a
clash, like blind moles" battling to death in a tunnel.[17] While group-
fantasy cycles in modern times are on the general order of four or five
years long, actual shooting wars occur only every fourth or fifth crisis,
when the psychological dynamics are right, the military preparations are
adequate, and when an "enemy" has been located who is at his own peak
of birth anxiety. Actually, statistical studies of wars confirm the lawful-
ness of this group process rather well, at least for most of the industrially-
developed world. In the past two centuries, for instance, wars have
occurred on the average of every 18 years in the U.S., 18 years in
England, 20 years in France, 24 years in Germany, and 18 years in
Russia.[16] Our ritual death-dance has a rhythm of its own which captures
every generation just as it reaches its peak of youth and then throws it
into the hellish maw of Moloch.

THE PERSONALITY OF PRESIDENTS

At this point, the reader is justified in stepping back and asking a
pertinent question: "If we grant that all the rather outrageous things you
have said so far have some measure of truth, and that so early an event as
birth seems to govern politics, then why bother with all the usual psychohistorical evidence about childhood and parental influence and personality development? It all appears quite hopeless the way you present
it—with these eternal cycles of birth and rebirth. What possible difference could it make *what* kind of personality the President has if politics
depends so much on birth experiences everyone shares?"

The answer is of course that birth is only a part of the story. Regardless of how traumatic an actual birth anyone has, even birth memories
are profoundly modified by later childhood experience. The more a child
is surrounded by love, freedom, and empathy, the more the child is able
to repeatedly rework its earliest anxieties, the more it is able to modify
them and even overcome them. A warm family provides a natural
therapy even for birth anxieties, and if, as I claim in my "Evolution of
Childhood" study,[18] childhood has a progressive trend throughout
history, mankind should eventually be able to cure itself of war just as it
has cured itself of slavery, vendetta, dueling, witchhunting and other
group-psychotic practices. Yet most children even today have simply
horrible childhoods, and wars are certain to continue for some time before

enough people become sufficiently emotionally mature not to need them. It is therefore one of our first tasks as psychohistorians to ask what kinds of personalities our leaders have and precisely how they interact with the emotional needs of the nation.

The psychohistorical study of presidential personality has unfortunately barely begun. There are only two Presidents who have been studied in sufficient depth, including their childhoods, to provide intelligent psychobiographies: Theodore Roosevelt and Richard Nixon.[19] Even so, enough information is available in primary sources to make a few generalizations about the kinds of people we have chosen to be our leaders in the twentieth century. First of all, none of them have had extremely traumatic childhoods. On the six-stage scale of family types which I use to measure childrearing modes (infanticidal, abandoning, ambivalent, intrusive, socializing, helping), all Presidents in this century fall into the next-to-highest "socializing mode" with the exception of Nixon, whose dour Quaker mother and often brutal father put his childhood in the lower "intrusive" category. What this means is that in order to become a leader of America today, you cannot have a background which includes continuous battering, repeated overt abandonment, or any other massively traumatic deprivations. (This, by the way, has *not* been the case for other countries and other periods—Hitler, for instance, was a classic "battered child", as were many of his generation of Austrians, the product of regular bloody beatings, hundreds of blows at a time.)[20] The overall level of American childhood, however, has been good enough in this century not to require such a psychopathic leader.

Within these limits, however, one trait stands out as common to the childhood of almost every President: an emotional distancing by the mother. This often occurs in the context of a series of nurses or other servants, to whom the mother delegates many of the child's caretaking functions, as was the case with T.R., F.D.R. and J.F.K.[21] It is as though the mothers of our Presidents must be "good enough" to give them the ego strength needed to survive the competition for leadership, but they must also be "distancing enough" to give them a deep hole of loneliness in the pit of their stomachs, a hole which they feel driven to fill with the needs and the adulation of large masses of people. No one who has not been the fantasy leader of an actual group can begin to image the demands put upon one who is expected to stay in touch with, and resolve, the deepest and most ambivalent anxieties of the "led." And generally only a deeply lonely person, who from childhood has expected to gain whatever approval and warmth he got by being the delegate of his mother's needs and by performing in perfect tune to her wishes, however distorted, can be expected to become a professional politician. The sight of our fantasy leaders following our emotional commands is so commonplace that we no longer even note it. David Frost tells Nixon on TV to make statesman-like noises, and he becomes the all-powerful leader of the free world. Frost tells him to "apologize to the people," and he cries and apologizes.

One childhood, however, stands out among those of all the Presidents for *not* having included a distancing mother: that of Dwight Eisenhower. Although no biographer has studied his childhood, scattered through his writings are enough references to his early years to make the psychohistorian prick up his ears and suspect that something was different here. Although he grew up at the turn of the century, and his father's occasional "application of leather" was similar to other families of the time, he had a most unusual mother, one whose closeness, warmth, consistency and real *happiness* with herself and her children was unique among the mothers of Presidents. Eisenhower's stories about her, even his use of adjectives, are quite unlike any other autobiographical writing I have encountered in any world leader. He speaks of her as "warm," "gentle," "serene," "tolerant," with "an open smile"—and gives enough detailed incidents to assure one that this is not a reaction formation. When she was put upon by others, she was capable of being thoroughly outraged and doing something about it (once, having been cheated out of something, she began to study law at home), and in general seemed unusually successful in "making life happy and meaningful for a family of eight," spending "many hours a day" with the children.[22] Her photographs are the only ones I have yet discovered in which the mother of a President is actually *smiling* (Eisenhower, too, is unique in smiling in his boyhood pictures, one happy face among his pained schoolboy comrades).

This unusual inner happiness made Eisenhower an oddball throughout his military career, from his early run-ins with the authoritarian MacArthur to his opposition to the rest of the military chiefs during World War Two with respect to the African landings (Eisenhower's plan for immediate invasion of France, which could have cut the war short by two years, was firmly overruled by Churchill).[23] But it was as President that Eisenhower was unique—so much so that it shows up plainly on our American group-fantasy graph (Chart A). Whereas other Presidents responded to the growing pressures of group-fantasy by finding a real war to act out, Eisenhower resisted all efforts to get him to be the usual fantasy leader. Although his political views were hardly unconventional, someplace deep inside him he found a core of maturity, and sense of personal worth, that enabled him to think rather than act when the majority of the country was saying: "We feel like we're dying—you must *do* something to relieve our fears." In fact, when he *did* act at the peak of two fantasy cycles, he did so in a way that at once relieved the anxieties by seeming to take war-like action but in no way actually led to war. The first was in 1955, when Congress—stung by his refusal to get into Indo-China—gave him a formal war-power resolution over Formosa, hoping he would get into a fight with China. But although Eisenhower spoke tough, he actually used U.S. forces only to *remove* Nationalist troops from the islands that were under contention, thus ending the crisis. And when the birth peak came again in 1958, he moved troops in and out of sleepy Lebanon in such a way as to make it appear that we had somehow won a victory against Communism. He did not achieve this war-free record easily—McCarthy was the spokesman of our frustration with Eisenhower's maturity—but he did so effectively. The point to remember is that it was one happy mother in Abilene, Kansas who, fifty years earlier, wrote the script for this most peaceful decade on the American historical stage.

THE PERSONALITY OF JIMMY CARTER

How, then, does Jimmy Carter's personality rate in comparison with other modern Presidents on the crucial parameters set out above? What kind of childhood did he have, what has his development been like to date, and what can his interactions with the American group-fantasy to date tell us about the likelihood that he will act out our next birth crisis in war-like action?

The available evidence on Carter's childhood which is presented in the following essays places him squarely with the majority of recent Presidents as the product of a "distancing" mother. For his mother worked much of the time, believed children should not be with their mothers very much, and delegated many of her caretaking functions to others. He of course adapted well to this initial emotional deprivation, as did other Presidents, but deep down inside there is a well of loneliness which has been the mainspring of his political career and the source for his oft-repeated and nearly mystical "intimate relationship with the American People." His meteoric rise from being "Jimmy Who?" to being President was based not on traditional machine politics but on a messianic "outsider" image, which was cultivated from the start to fill whatever group-fantasies Americans projected into him. (Pat Caddell's famous memo to Carter—which told him that the fact that people do not know what Carter stands for is an *asset* because "large parts of the electorate can project their own desires on to Gov. Carter"—is as good a definition of the fantasy leader as I have seen.)[24] In particular, as David Beisel analyzes in detail in his study, Carter won the election through his intimate variations on themes taken from the Watergate loss of leadership, themes which drew on elements of his personal history, the myth of his "perfect" family, and the nation's feeling of having been "abandoned" by their deposed leader. His personality has every trait seen in that of our past war leaders. His experience in childhood in interpreting his mother's distanced and often distorted messages made him extremely sensitive to the hidden group-fantasy needs of the nation; his need to live up to both his parents' seemingly unfulfillable expectations made him a classic workaholic; and both his populist image and his choice of an "active-positive" political role tend to make him action-prone when the time comes to carry out a birth episode. His positions on war to date have been consistent with that of a future wartime leader. He was a Vietnam hawk up to the end of the war, and ever since then the topic of world peace has rarely been mentioned by him as an overriding goal of his Presidency.

There is nothing, I believe, which he has done since his inauguration to offset this summary of personality traits. He began by choosing his foreign policy staff out of the Rockefeller-supported Trilateral Commission, he has cooled down relations with Russia, scrapped years of effort in disarmament, discovered a "12-year decline" in NATO armament, urged a new push to build up NATO forces, scrapped his promise to reduce the American arms budget, and—lest the quiet, steady, insistent growth of atomic weaponry be completely forgotten—has added even more atomic warheads to the tens of thousands which presently exist, many of them in the new "more acceptable" form of battlefield atomic weaponry. That this new mood of belligerence has been virtually unnoted by the liberal press is to be expected—psychohistorians have learned to read *U.S. News and World Report,* not the *New York Times,* to find out what is really going on in American group-fantasy. The headlines of a recent issue of *U.S. News* in fact read: "THE PRESIDENT TALKS TOUGH . . . Harder Line With Russia," and quotes Carter as follows:

Africa:	"We see the possibility of war in the southern part of Africa as being ever-present."
Mideast:	"Americans would not respond well to any overt or implied threats" of an oil embargo.
Panama Canal:	"There is a potential threat to the Canal. . ."
Soviet Union:	"The differences between us and the Soviet Union are still wide and very significant."[25]

(The *New York Times,* the same week, took an astonishing report from its Mideast expert, Drew Middleton, headlined "Two Sides in Middle East Speak Casually of a War As Stress Shifts From Political to Military Solution," and buried it in the inner pages instead of giving it the first-page treatment it obviously merited.)[26]

Carter's language, as revealed by extensive Fantasy Analysis of his speeches, is quietly permeated with the imagery of fear and war. When it occurs in the context of a domestic issue, so that an energy program becomes "the moral equivalent of war," the press picks up and repeats the imagery, with headlines about a world-wide oil crisis that requires "wartime urgency"[27] and cartoons showing Carter dressed as Jesus walking with a sign saying "The End Is Near." When his speech is about foreign matters, it bristles with the same kind of aggressive and fearful imagery, carefully hidden between noble phrases, that I have found time and again in Fantasy Analyses of Presidential speeches before other war-like actions. Here, for instance, is a Fantasy Analysis of his Notre Dame University address on May 22, 1977:

> dark faith . . . strands that connect . . . confidence . . . separated . . . strength . . . arms . . . fear . . . fear . . . fought fire with fire . . . fire is better fought with water . . . confidence . . . contained . . . weakened its foundation . . . war . . . crisis . . . sapping . . . strains . . . weakened . . . crisis . . . danger . . . violence . . . combat . . . fear . . . awakening . . . powerful . . . strong . . . war . . . reduce the chase . . . war . . . hatred . . . damage, hunger and disease . . . blood . . . despair . . . reinforce the bonds . . . confidence . . . dangerous . . . freeze . . . weapons . . . attack . . . death . . . explosives . . . military intervention . . . military force . . . danger . . . arms . . . explosives . . . explosives . . . arms . . . arms . . . war[28]

That there is a positive side to many of Carter's words and actions which lead to increasing tensions is of course not to be denied. But that he has a deeply-felt commitment to human rights, for instance, does not negate the fact that the *form* and particularly the *timing* of his repeated attacks on Russia with respect to human rights are part of the "get tough" fantasy, and incidentally do nothing for the Russian dissidents he is defending. The same case could be made for the form and timing of his statements on Palestine, Africa, and so on.

What is more, the American public is, I think, fully aware of the hidden imagery of Jimmy Carter as a future war-leader. His leading symbol—his teeth—is the identical image regularly used in portraying another leader chosen for his belligerence, Theodore Roosevelt, especially in his "Big Stick," aggressive, "biting" role.[29] Even Carter's ambiguity as to whether he is a liberal or a conservative acts to increase tensions. For Carter is an ideal President to obstruct. Conservatives can oppose him as a Democrat, Liberals as a Conservative, and it seems a good bet that stalemate will be the main theme of the period in 1978 while stage three builds up—as it often is in other stage three periods—and that the peak of tensions for stage four will, if the past two decades is any guide, occur some time in 1979.

Given the current condition of the Middle East as the world's tender-box, and given the current American view that any future oil embargo is a crucial "strangulating" birth precipitant, one is even tempted to fore-cast the scene of the next conflict. Henry Kissinger has declared that America will go to war in the Middle East only "where there is some actual strangulation." Gerald Ford has said: "In the case of economic strangulation we must be prepared to take the necessary action for our self-preservation. When you are being strangled it is a case of either dying or living." (Ford's definition of "strangulation" is even more fetal: "Strangulation, if you translate it into the terms of a human being, means that you are just about on your back.")[30] I need hardly say that when I begin to hear the word "strangulation" bandied about regularly some time in 1979, I intend to put my family and dog in the car and head for Canada, out of the way of the prevailing winds and atomic fallout.

Even if the hairline trigger of the Mideast is not the actual release mechanism for the next crisis, it is doubtful that anything short of war-like action will be the stage upon which the drama is played. While the conditions that determine whether a birth-crisis takes the form of war, revolution, or other leadership crisis are yet to be presented, Carter's personality seems to be quite closed to precipitation of a leadership crisis like Nixon's. Nor does he have the kind of self-destructive drive and accident-proneness which made Kennedy go into Dallas while full-page ads were using the language of violence, and then ride slowly through the center of town in an open car. So the only thing that can deter Carter from responding to our next call for war, when "pressures" once again grow intolerable, is his maturity.

Might Carter's well-known "independence" include an independence even from us? Might a man who can show physical warmth to his wife in public—and mean it—be able to tap some deep source of human warmth in his heart when the chips are down and decline to plunge us into another hellish birth? Might a man who spends whole days with his daughter, in which she plans every minute of his time, be able to remem-ber that children really die in wars?

One hopes so. For on such a slender thread of hope hangs the existence of mankind.

Lloyd deMause is Director of The Institute for Psychohistory, Editor of The Journal of Psychohistory, *publisher of The Psychohistory Press, a member of the training faculty of the New York Center of Psycho-analytic Training, chairman of the International Pscyhohistorical Asso-ciation, and editor and an author of* The History of Childhood, A Bibliography of Psychohistory, *and* The New Psychohistory.

REFERENCES

1. Some recent psychohistorical studies which attempt to capture stages of national fantasy include Lloyd deMause, "Formation of the American Personality Through Psychospeciation" *The Journal of Psychohistory* 4 (1976): 1-30; Rudolph Binion, *Hitler Among the Germans.* New York: Elsevier, 1977; Lloyd deMause, ed. *The New Psychohistory.* New York: The Psychohistory Press, 1975; and Glenn Davis, *Childhood and History in America.* New York: The Psychohistory Press, 1976.

2. The twenty-two projects sponsored by The Institute for Psychohistory to date are: the history of childhood project (Lloyd deMause and others); the new psychohistory project (Lloyd deMause and others); the childhood and history in America project (Glenn Davis); the Hitler psychobiography project (Helm Stierlin); the Carter project (this volume); the Anglo-American family cycle project (Martin Quitt and Vivian Fox); the *Journal of Psychological Anthropology* project (Arthur Hippler and others); the English martyrdom project (Seymour Byman); the psychohistory of American education project (Barbara Finkelstein and others); the American millenarianism project (Joseph Dowling); the psychocultural evolution project (Arthur Hippler); the fetal origins of history project (Lloyd deMause); the Virginia colonial history project (Martin Quitt); the first millenarian movement project (Henry Ebel); the psychohistory of modern social services project (Henry Lawton); the psychohistory as a profession project (Rudolph Binion and others); the frontier family project (Alice Eichholz); the evolution of historical personality project (deMause); the German nationalism project (David Beisel); the transference problems in psychohistorians project (Paul Elovitz); the small group process project (John Hartman); the Bismark psychohistory project (Jacques Szaluta).

3. For my theory of historical group-fantasy, see Lloyd deMause, "The Psychogenic Theory of History" *The Journal of Psychohistory* 4 (1977): 253-267. For its application to war, see Lloyd deMause "The Independence of Psychohistory" *The Journal of Psychohistory* 3 (1975): 163-183 and Lloyd deMause "Formation of the American Personality." For a recent bibliography on political socialization, see Fred I. Greenstein and Michael Lerner, eds. *A Source Book for the Study of Personality and Politics.* Chicago: Markham Publishing, 1971.

4. Lloyd deMause, "The Fetal Origins of History" *The Journal of Psychohistory* (forthcoming).

5. Reviews of the World Situation, 1949-1950. Hearings Held in Executive Session Before the Senate Committee on Foreign Relations,

U.S. Senate, Eighty-First Congress, First Session. Washington, D.C.: U.S. Government Printing Office, 1974.

6. For a review and bibliography of the literature of the body memory of birth and its relationship to history, see the Special Birth Issue of *The Journal of Psychohistory* (Winter 1977, Vol. 4, No. 3), especially the articles by myself, Stanislav Grof, Leslie Feher, Francis J. Mott, Henry Ebel, Alice Eichholz and Henry Lawton. For my theory of the fetal origins of history, see my studies cited in footnotes 3 and 4 above.

7. For the story of how psychohistorians predicted this October, 1973 Red Alert and their denial of its happening, see Lloyd deMause, "Psychohistory and Psychotherapy" 2(1975): 408-414.

8. "Polls in Perspective: Carter—A Popular President, But—" *U.S. News and World Report,* May 30, 1977, p. 24.

9. See my "Psychogenic Theory" and "Fetal Origins" articles for details on the fetal trance state.

10. One perceptive political psychologist calls this group trance state "groupthink"; see Irving L. Janis, *Victims of Groupthink: A Psychological Study of Foreign Policy Decisions and Fiascoes.* Boston: Houghton, Mifflin, 1972. Another political psychologist has even measured a sort of paranoia index through content-analysis of language used just prior to World War I; see Ole R. Holsti and Robert C. North "The History of Human Conflict" in Elton B. McNeil, ed. *The Nature of Human Conflict.* Englewood Cliffs, Prentice-Hall, 1965, p. 166.

11. deMause, "Independence of Psychohistory", pp. 172-182.

12. deMause, "Formation of the American Personality", pp. 13-15.

13. The German quote is from Max Montgelas and Walter Schucking, eds. *Outbreak of the World War: German Documents Collected By Karl Kautsky.* New York: Oxford University Press, 1924, p. 307. The Nixon quote is from the *New York Times,* September 19, 1962, p. 3.

14. Bert Cochran. *Harry Truman and the Crisis Presidency.* New York: Funk and Wagnalls, 1973, p. 316.

15. Dean G. Acheson. *Present at the Creation: My Years in the State Department.* New York: Norton, 1969, p. 220.

16. Maurice N. Walsh, ed. *War and the Human Race.* New York: Elsevier, 1971, p. 78.

17. Robert F. Kennedy. *Thirteen Days: A Memoir of the Cuban Missile Crisis.* New York: W.W. Norton, 1966, p. 89.

18. Lloyd deMause, "The Evolution of Childhood" in deMause, ed. *The History of Childhood.* New York: The Psychohistory Press, 1974.

19. See Glenn Davis, "Theodore Roosevelt and the Progressive Era: A Study in Individual and Group Psychohistory" in deMause, ed.

The New Psychohistory. New York: Psychohistory Press, 1975, pp. 245-305. For Nixon, see both James W. Hamilton, "Some Reflections on Richard Nixon in the Light of His Resignation and Farewell Speeches" *The Journal of Psychohistory* 4(1977):491-511 and David Abrahamson, *Nixon vs Nixon: An Emotional Tragedy.* New York: Farrar, Straus, Giroux, 1977. Other "psychobiographies" have little childhood information, and cannot be seriously considered as professionally adequate psychobiographies. Doris Kearns' *Lyndon Johnson and the American Dream,* for instance, depended entirely on Johnson's account of his childhood, with no attempt at any independent research into primary sources. Bruce Mazlish's *In Search of Nixon* was written, he himself has said, only after proper funding was denied him to do a thorough job of going to Whittier to dig out the facts on his childhood. Nancy Gager Clinch's *The Kennedy Neurosis* has one page on JFK's severe childhood discipline, but again attempts no independent research into the sources. Freud's book on Wilson is a disaster. And so on. It will be years before even a start is made on forming any general opinions on the personalities of American Presidents.

20. See Rudolph Binion, *Hitler Among the Germans.* New York: Elsevier, 1976; Helm Stierlin, *Adolf Hitler: A Family Perspective.* New York: Psychohistory Press, 1977; Robert Waite, *The Psychopathic God: Adolf Hitler.* New York: Basic Books, 1977.

21. Glenn Davis, *Childhood and History in America.* New York: Psychohistory Press, 1976.

22. Dwight D. Eisenhower. *At Ease: Stories I Tell to Friends.* Garden City: Doubleday & Co., 1967, pp. 32-37, 76.

23. Peter Lyon. *Eisenhower: Portrait of the Hero.* Boston: Little, Brown & Co., 1974, pp. 78, 128ff.

24. Caddell is quoted in Henry Fairlie, "Sweet Nothings" *The New Republic,* June 11, 1977, p. 18.

25. U.S. News & World Report, June 6, 1977, pp. 17, 19.

26. *New York Times,* June 7, 1977, p. 3.

27. *New York Post,* May 16, 1977, p. 1.

28. *New York Times,* May 23, 1977, p. 12.

29. See especially the "Teeth" cartoons of T.R. in Stephen Hess and Milton Kaplan, *The Ungentlemanly Art: A History of American Political Cartoons.* Rev. Ed. New York: Macmillan, 1975, p. 130.

30. Ford quotes in Terence McCarthy, "The Middle East: Will We Go To War?" *Ramparts,* April 1977, p. 21.

CHAPTER TWO

Three Days in Plains

PAUL H.
ELOVITZ

The last thing I did before leaving for Plains, Georgia on October 26, 1976, was to discuss with my colleagues my feelings toward Southerners, the Carters, and politicians in general. I am a Northerner, a psychotherapist, and a college teacher. Why should these people bother talking to me, especially when I felt such difference/superiority/ prejudice toward what they represented? And since I had only three days in Plains in which to accomplish my work, could there be any rational prognosis of success?

As it turned out, the realities of what I was able to accomplish far exceeded my expectations. Carter's black childhood "nanny," Annie Mae Jones, gave me an interview; so did his sister Gloria; and my extended conversation with his mother, Lillian, even included her feeding me dinner. In addition, I was able to interview A. D. Davis, Jimmy's black childhood friend, to photograph materials left by Jimmy's elementary school teacher, Julia Coleman, at the time of her death in 1973, to photograph part of Jimmy's Annapolis autobiography, and to speak to a number of Plains residents who also provided helpful information.

Of course, I did other things in attempting to immerse myself in the Carter "milieu." I bought peanuts (boiled in salt) and sugar cane from a black vendor, thus sharing the tastes of Carter's childhood. I walked the tracks in front of his childhood home, picking up the types of stones he might have used in his flip or slingshot. I visited his family cemetery. And I sampled as much as I could bear of the new mythology already under construction in the town, including a bus tour set up by an enterprising local college teacher.

LILLIAN CARTER

I met Lillian Carter at one p.m. on my first day of interviewing. She was "receiving" at the train station, and despite the stress of having to acknowledge hundreds of visitors, was extraordinarily pleasant to me. Dynamic, small, 78 years old—a controlling personality—yet too fragile to actually shake hands with all of her well-wishers. As people move towards her she is quick to say "Don't shake my hand," but does it in a way that is usually inoffensive. Watching all the pushing, pulling and shoving that was going on around her, I felt keenly how difficult this must be for anyone to endure over long periods of time, as in a presidential campaign. On the spur of the moment, Lillian said yes, she would give me an interview when she had finished at the train station and an appointment with her hairdresser. "You know a woman has to have her hair done. You wouldn't want me not to have my hair done, would you?"

The overwhelming impression I had during my hours with her in her Plains home was one of contradictory messages—of being placed, almost, in an on-going "double bind" by the fact that what she was saying to me had a hidden edge at variance with her overt meaning. Some of this may have been due to my own unfamiliarity with the limits and conventions of Southern hospitality. (How many times should I be offered dinner before accepting the invitation as genuine?) But much of it was clearly more habitual and more deeply rooted than such considerations would imply. Thus, jokes about my leaving were coupled with the statement that "I don't want to rush you" and with invitations to dinner, as well as the (joking) suggestion that I might consider staying overnight. And despite the pressures of the election, which included telephone calls from as far as Australia, she seemed very eager to please me, and to help me finish my work.

Lillian clearly felt bombarded, and complained of "all these telephone calls I get each day, and my mind is always on something else." Moments later she declared: "Oh, I'm completely relaxed"—when in fact she so clearly *wasn't* relaxed. She gave me her new phone number; the old one had had to be changed because there were just too many calls flooding in, to some extent because of her habit of telling people to "be sure to call me."

She complained almost bitterly about a manuscript sent her by a woman in California who wanted her "to read it, write a foreword to it —to tell how much I enjoyed it. You know, I wouldn't get around to this until after Christmas." Then she added that when she goes to California she would like to "drop the manuscript off sheet by sheet," and left me with the feeling that she would read it through and, quite possibly, write the introduction.

Early in the interview she touched on the unkind letters she had received that morning. "But they're all opposition, started by somebody on the other side." She was quite sensitive to criticism. An association popped into my mind: the tension of a woman who rejects the pretensions and materialistic priorities of "well-off-people," but drives Cadillacs and Lincolns and has declared that "my car is my one luxury"; who lives in comfortable and sometimes affluent homes, but likes to keep house without a live-in maid.

When I declared my interest in Jimmy's childhood, Lillian's reply was straightforward: "I can tell you anything you want to know." My expectations soared—unrealistically, as it turned out. She seemed much more interested in talking about her daughter Gloria. "Anyone who gets an interview with Gloria has struck a gold mine. I'll tell you what—listen— I've told several people, not everyone, that she has no active part in any of this—but she is the most brilliant child I have, and I have four brilliant children. And Jimmy would tell you that Gloria is the most brilliant when he is speaking confidentially about it."

She noted that she had saved all of Jimmy's schoolwork, but none of the letters and "things" sent by Ruth and Gloria when they were away— and attributed her behavior to "a mother's premonition." She gave the general impression that when speaking of her children's early experiences and her own influence on them she is very defensive.

She had strong, positive feelings about her husband, but interspersed with an occasional apologetic note. "Everything that I ever did to anyone, my husband backed me one hundred percent. My husband was the strong one in the family. He was the boss. He was the head of the family and I never did anything that he didn't want me to do. If I did, I had to apologize—or I was in trouble. I've apologized to him many a time when I felt like it was his fault. To keep the peace and the harmony of the family. But my children took after him as much as they did me."

Explanations followed: Earl had very bad eyes, yet read a lot, and "you just had to wear thick glasses if you had bad eyes . . . and everything I did in the way of being liberal, as people called me, he backed me fully and he financed it—everything I did, and fully. Billy looks like my husband—very much looks like him—and I think that Billy is more like him except that Billy drinks too much beer, and I think that maybe

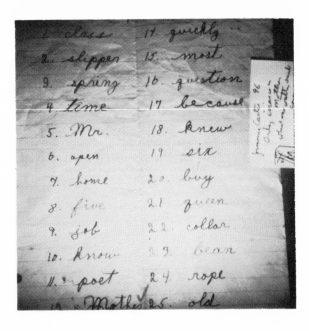

Fig. 1. A grade-school notebook of Jimmy Carter, with the correction "Mother" for "mother."

Fig. 2. Jimmy Carter's childhood home in Archery, Georgia.

Fig. 3. A typical Georgia shanty of the last generation, located near the Carters' "Pond House." Most have now been destroyed.

Fig. 4. Jimmy Carter, in a scrapbook kept by Julia Coleman in 1939-40.

Fig. 5. Jimmy Carter's high-school biology club. His photograph appears in the lower row, the second picture left of center.

Fig. 6. Lillian Carter's living-room.

Fig. 7. The room at the Wise Sanatorium in which Jimmy Carter was born.

Fig. 8. Psychohistorian Paul Elovitz with Carter's childhood "nanny," Annie Mae Jones.

Fig. 9. Earl Carter.

Fig. 10. Jimmy Carter as a teen-ager.

Fig. 11. Rosalynn Carter as a 7th Grader.

Fig. 12. Jimmy Carter and his schoolmates (Carter at lower right).

Fig. 13. From the scrapbook of Jimmy Carter's high-school teacher, Julia Coleman: "12 Great Books—'Readers Make Leaders'."

Fig. 14. From the scrapbook of Julia Coleman: the "Book Lovers Club," with Jimmy Carter's photograph at right center.

Gloria has a lot of Earl in her, but Jimmy, everything except for brilliance, he gets from me. I think that we're more alike.''

Then: "I don't think any more of Jimmy than I do of Billy. I'm just as proud of Billy as I am of Jimmy, although they're too different people.''

Lillian has emphatic opinions on civil rights for blacks. Earlier in the conversation she commented caustically on "dressed-up" people, many from the North, who try to get ahead of the blacks on line in order to shake her hand. "You know, some people come in with the idea that we are—that this is a hick town, and that 'We're from the North and we're very wealthy.' I see them coming in Lincolns and every kind . . . and I say, 'I'm sorry, honey, I see you're not in line. You have to get to the *back* of the line.' And why, they resent more than anything if you have black people in the line.'' Now her conversation turns to the same subject in association with her most famous son. "You know, down here—and I don't want to get into civil rights, I don't want to get into that here, that's all closed now and I want peace. But when Jimmy was a young boy we had a lot of black people living on our farm—we all loved them—they helped me raise the children. Jimmy's playmate was a little black boy, as you heard. Gloria's was a little black girl. We didn't have anybody white near us in the country. And [Jimmy's] compassion is right on the same plane as mine.''

She continues: "I had been a nurse, but I kept my registration up for years and years because I was able to do so much for people in a nursing way—in a medical way—and when we had sadness among the blacks, Jimmy would go with me. He was just as compassionate. When we had someone die he would go with me. We would attend the funeral. He always—he would always want to go with me. He did that just because he was so compassionate. My husband was very compassionate but he didn't want to go to a black funeral. People just didn't do that. Just Jimmy and me, mostly. But I think all of my children inherited my compassion.''

She moved on to a subject later to become familiar to students of her granddaughter Amy's deportment. "I was an avid reader. I read all the time and my children—I didn't teach them to read—they took a lesson from me. They watched me read and they naturally wanted to read. So all my children read all the time, and they took advantage of me about that. When I would say, 'Jimmy, what are you doing?'—I wanted him to do a chore for me—and he would say, 'I'm just reading, what do you want, mama?' And I'd say, 'Go ahead.' And I said, 'Gloria, what are you doing?' and she said 'I'm reading, mother. I'm in my room.' And then I'd go do it, don't you see? Of course, they were older than the other two children, but you asked me who they were like, and all I could tell you is Jimmy and I have always been able to talk freely to each other, to discuss different things and to accept politics.''

Abruptly, she mentioned childhood notebooks and an Annapolis diary. Jimmy's. Some had already been photographed under the direction of "Mr. Kirbo." I became extremely excited, and slowly overcame her hesitations by reiterating my credentials as a college professor. Did I have photographic equipment? (Yes.) "I'm going to do that. I'm going to leave you here to do that because I have other chores to do in town. Someone will be coming with a package." And in a minute, she was gone. I felt precisely like a starving child who has been handed a cookie jar. Jimmy's seventh-grade workbook had such utter gems as "Good health is clean teeth" and, under the heading *Healthy Mental Habits*: "There are certain other habits of thinking which have a good effect upon health. If you think in the right way, you'll develop: 1) the habit of expecting to accomplish what you attempt, 2) the habit of expecting to like other people and to have them like you, and 3) the habit of deciding quickly what you'd like to do and doing it, 4) the habit of sticking to it, 5) the habit of welcoming fearfully [sic] all wholesome ideas and experiences." Number 6 branched off into a mini-essay: "A person who wants to build good mental habits should avoid the idle daydream; should give up worry and anger; hatred and envy; should neither fear nor be ashamed of anything that is honest or purposeful.''

And on one early school paper was the notation that Jimmy spelled "mother" with a lower-case "m" in cases that required a capital letter.

From the Annapolis diary: "On Thursday night I cut my hand on a broken cup at the table & had to have 2 stitches taken in it. I got on the excused squad because I couldn't wear a glove, and it wasn't so bad. Daddy got up here Friday night and I saw him for about a half hour then. Met him Saturday & at noon meal formation (which he saw) we ate out. We went to a show after chow & then walked around town & the yard. I was really glad to see him & enjoyed learning about home. Billy has the mumps he said. Dined out with him . . . Wynne had me calling cadence & beat me with a klak. Not too bad. Been having three speeches per meal in Bull, & I'm really tired of them. I cut my gums this morning at table & as it was bleeding I didn't have to speak. I think it was worth it.''

All of this in extra-large handwriting—which at this point grows smaller. "Up until tonight there's been nothing of interest. I still haven't been fried yet, but have been around several times lately. The musical club show will be the 19th of this month . . . '' In skimming the diary I saw no earlier reference to parental visits to Annapolis. The entire diary had a manic or "racing" tone to it. The thought crossed my mind, with respect to that accidental or willful slashing of his gums, that Jimmy was hurting himself in part to lessen the pain of military discipline, and that the man who might be President—and for whom I would probably be voting in a few days—might have a self-destructive streak.

Meanwhile, Lillian had returned to the house, and was watching "M.A.S.H." on television while eating her dinner. "If there's nothing on Rosalynn, you can copy anything" was her reply to one of my anxious questions. But over the next few hours there followed four or five comments to the effect that "I really shouldn't trust you—but I am." Our intermittent conversation became punctuated with offers of food, and the third time around I accepted. She declined my offer to help with the cooking, and I went back to my photographic work. She brought me a plate with a large hamburger on it, helped me clear the table, then took her own plate and marched back to the living room to eat separately from me. "You can just keep on working while you're eating." But the separation was inconclusive. From the living room came apologies for the fact that the TV set was only a black-and-white—the color TV was "out at the Pond house"—and a series of reappearances. "Do you want some Twinkies? They're really so good." Protestations about my diet were unavailing. She gave me the Twinkies and I dutifully ate them. "Can I give you a beer? I've got beer in the refrigerator. I hate beer. They belong to the security man upstairs. I don't know if he'd mind if you drank one. I hate beer." And comparable episodes: Would you like it?—it isn't mine—but would you like to have it anyway?—I don't like it myself—but you can have it. The net result was that I did not feel comfortable, and found myself wondering what the effect of this kind of continuous ambivalence could be on one's children.

The announcement that her secretary would soon stop by brought more ambivalence to the fore. "She doesn't have a bit of sense," Lillian complained, and "I can't trust her with anything"—but she was obviously trusting her to help with the mail. The secretary turned out to be a pleasant and very businesslike young woman, who left soon after Lillian gave her some materials to work on. And there was no hint of ambivalence as long as Lillian was relating to her directly.

Lillian often spoke as if she were a woman with almost no power over her own life. At the same time, the lines of people filing past her rocking chair were an eloquent tribute to her powers of control, and at such moments she herself exudes a sense of being in her glory. On the other hand, she typically works "through" an all-powerful male, be it her husband Earl, her son Jimmy, or the physician under whose supervision she worked as a Peace Corps volunteer in India. Much of her complaining, indeed, seems to stem from the self-imposed requirement that she live up to an image she has helped to create.

A little after eight in the evening, she came in from the living room, and we started a conversation about her experiences in India. She was standing in the doorway as we began, but then pulled up a chair, and instead of putting it on my side of the doorway, put it down on the far side, in the hall area, so that a third of her face and body was blocked by the doorpost. At the same time, at this comfortable distance, her comments, and the way she expressed them, were fascinating. She described her despair about India—how bad things had gotten—and communicated feelings of extreme depression and defeat. It felt very much like a therapy situation—even the oblique relationship to me seemed reminiscent of the classic use of the couch in psychoanalysis. She said that letters had come daily from her children, begging her to come home from India before it ruined her health and life—"before it killed me" was the unspoken implication I caught. At this point she said she had spoken to God—"the way [my daughter] Ruth would speak to God" —as if he were just another person sitting in front of her. She said, according to her own account: "God, I've got to be able to do it. I've got to be able to help. And do you know, the next day a man came from the doctor [asking that she serve as his assistant]. My prayer had been answered." I shared her elation at this triumph.

Her conversation turned to the only painting Jimmy had ever done. "Rosalynn paints, but it's the only painting Jimmy ever did. He did it when he was at Schenectady. Oh, there's a mark here. I told the man who framed it he should take it away—he should clean this out—there's a piece of sand—you see it thee?" Meanwhile I was thinking: My God— what utter despair—such a bare, windswept painting. Four trees stood out, three of them almost levelled by the wind, one straight, with a bit of water and a boat, a mountain, and an overwhelming greyness. I thought of the four children in the Carter family. Lillian must have seen the expression in my eyes because she quickly said: "Look here—there's some green." And she pointed to one small patch that did seem less grey and dreary. The painting was done when he was well launched on his career and working for Admiral Rickover. Perhaps it was less the pull of his home town that brought him back from the Navy than the feelings expressed in this painting—and publicly denied in his admiration for such an ungiving, unbending boss.

The painting left me a bit shaken. I became suddenly concerned with my room reservations for that night, and called my motel. The experience suddenly seemed so draining that I determined to finish up with the materials I had on the table, at the risk of missing some valuable item still in storage elsewhere in the house. While her secretary was still present Lillian had joked about my staying the night, a joke she echoed several times in our subsequent conversation, but I had the sense that she really *was* inviting me to sleep over—that despite her having to get up early, make arrangements, and leave for the campaign, and all her articulated upsets about the pressures on her time, she enjoyed my presence. And I found that I had entered my own spiral of ambivalence, feeling a great deal of sympathy for her—she seemed so small and frail, and was I keeping her up too late?—while feeling that I just had to get away from all these exhausting worries and emotions. I kissed her on the forehead and asked that she let me find my own way out. But she followed and saw me to the door.

GLORIA CARTER SPANN

When Lillian was still finishing up at the train station and having her hair done, I called her daughter Gloria. Yes, this was Gloria. Yes, she had gotten my letter. No, she couldn't see me—and proceeded to give me reason after reason as to why this was the case. In utter panic, I reacted as I do as a therapist and agreed with the resistance. Yes, she must be swamped. Yes, she had to prepare for the party and the auction weekend. But in between I sandwiched the fact that nothing would go into print until after the election. After more conversation of this sort she asked where I was and said: "You just wait right there—I'll be there in five minutes, if you don't mind interviewing me while I go to the food store." (It later turned out that she felt her husband would disapprove if she allowed the interview to take place in her home.)

She was very defensive in the car, hiding behind her sunglasses and reluctant to smile, and insisting that her standard interview technique was only to confirm or deny the correctness of statements made by the interviewer. Fortunately, this phase was brief, and we gradually talked more freely. Small talk at first, about the trees she would climb as a young girl, in Jimmy's company, about how her parents never told her not to climb. Jimmy and Gloria had set up a whole system of economics based on chinaberry money. The image she presented of her childhood was an extremely happy one, with Jimmy cast at times in a Huck Finn role, but at all times as a bossy older brother. He had paid her a nickel at one time for picking peanuts on his behalf, then got her to plant it in a flower bed, as the prelude to a "money tree," and dug it up himself. He was able to do this repeatedly, "but I didn't realize that for a long time. That's it," she observed with an air of finality, "when we were in school he was just a big brother and I was a little sister and he didn't pay any attention to me at school if he could possibly help it. A typical boy."

I was struck by the difference between this picture and that presented in Carter's autobiography. Gloria, he writes there, was two years younger "but larger during our growing years," their father's favorite, and always getting Jimmy into trouble. Gloria's comments implicitly denied any favoritism on Earl's part. My inquiries about the role of Annie Mae Jones elicited the sense of a black nurse who was protective but also a source of fear. "She taught us the old folk songs and the tales.

That there was a boogie man who lived about a hundred yards from the house. So there never was any thought of running away from home at night. There was also an old bloody ghost that walked the railroad tracks right in front of our house. So we never went on the railroad tracks.''

At the same time, Gloria denied these childhood terrors. "Yes, but it didn't really scare us, you know. I mean, it didn't do a thing. I think that would be the best thing for the young people today, to revive the boogie man [laughing]. And naturally, [Annie Mae] had lots of little tales about not working on Sundays and not going to church on Sunday. That was a part of their lives and a part of our lives, and we grew up 'bi-lingual' by that meaning. I mean, if you could get into the environment of Plains you'd find that everybody who grew up in this area speaks the black dialect, and it would be impossible for you to understand the native blacks who are over forty years old who have not been educated away from here. That's something that I don't think many of us ever give a thought to.'' She stressed that the black dialect wasn't pidgin English. It was just "different words."

She returned to the theme of fear—specifically, a cemetery that she and Jimmy often passed on the way to and from Plains, and a house that had the reputation of being haunted. "So when we'd get to the edge of the cemetery, we'd get off the bicycle, and I'd take one handlebar and he'd take the other. We'd shut our eyes and run. Boy, it was scary. We'd do the same with the haunted house.'' She said they had continued to do so until Jimmy was twelve and could start driving.

We soon got onto the subject of schooling in Plains, and the influence on Jimmy of Julia Coleman. "Jimmy 'studied hard' in that he didn't really study. He didn't have to study. He was smart in high school and made excellent grades and he was definitely in the top one percent of his class all through school.'' She pictured the school system as one of high quality, mainly through the influence of Miss Coleman, who was "just an excellent English teacher'' and who bought books for the children out of her own money. Schooling was highly competitive, and all sorts of certificates were given out based on the number of books read—twenty books (verified by book reports) meant a bronze medal on graduation night. Gloria and Jimmy still had theirs.

For the Carter children, school opened up, among other things, a whole world of classical music and painting. Gloria remembered herself, most typically, as writing essays, and Jimmy as being on the debating team, the basketball team, and the baseball team, and, in one year, as the school "spinning champion.''

Jimmy's close friends? "Yes, all boys in his class were Jimmy's close friends. They still are—like Rembert Forrest of Long Island, New York.'' She also pictured Jimmy as a boy who "never did get into any kind of trouble.'' We then got sidetracked into a conversation about Norman

Mailer, and agreed that we did not like Mailer's article on Carter despite its favorable outlook on her brother. "Now, if I had written one of Mailer in Plains, and the reaction several people had to this lady he was sleeping with, that would have been really terrific." About her correspondence with Edward Diamond, the co-author of an earlier study of Carter, she said: "I'll never open up my mouth again since he did that psychohistory thing."

As I pondered the ethics of *not* telling her that I am myself a psychohistorian, she looked over at me and said: "Are you Jewish?" I answered in the affirmative. "Well, it's impossible for a Yankee Jew to psychoanalyze the religion of a Southern Baptist fundamentalist, and it struck me as funny that they [Mazlish and Diamond] did it, and they did such a beautiful job. And I wrote them and told them that there were some very simple terms that they could have used, that the most illiterate person in one of the churches would have known down here, without them going into all those great big words."

Where her parents were concerned, Gloria revealed a very defensive feeling about her father and almost a nostalgic feeling toward Lillian—a feeling particularly that her mother's true personality was getting lost in the campaign. "She's beneath it [sic] even though she's marvelous, and she does come through. At times, when she rebels for her own self, it's misinterpreted. Yet, as for herself alone—and it's been this way for a long time, since, I guess since Jimmy was running for governor after she came home from the Peace Corps—this has been a kind of thing in the whole family—it's almost as if she's given her whole life to this family."

When we touched on her father, Gloria was close to anger at the notion that her father was a harsh, child-beating racist. Her comments carried the sense of Earl as a harsh, child-beating racist. She did review all the things Earl had done for his children—a tennis court, the pond house—and noted with respect to Jimmy that "he was punished only six times"—the precise count contrasting oddly with the intent of her statement—"and that was the only punishment he got other than restrictions. Now as we got older, being strict was 'You can't have a date for two weeks' or 'You can't have the car for a month.' That was if we stayed out late or caused them any anxiety or [Gloria's Emphasis] *sassed my mother—which was the worst thing that we could do—talk back to my mother.* And so we had the same punishment until the time I was twelve years old. My punishment was switching, and switching was with a light peach-tree switch that was by far the most preferable punishment." Because it was over with fast? "Yes, then it was done. The worst punishment that could happen to us would be for Daddy to go out on the front porch and call one of us by our name. My daddy never called us by our name unless it was something very serious, and that meant he was going to ask us about something that we knew we had done already, and he was going to give us a lecture. Oh, that was horrible. It really was, because he was dead serious, and I couldn't stand it. And I still can't."

Did these lectures last very long? "No, it usually wouldn't be very long. It would be right before your lunch—test your appetite. But then it would be over with. Say I'm sorry and I'll never do it again. It was the same with the dance we did when we got the switching—the 'I ain't gonna do it no more, I ain't gonna do it no more, I ain't gonna do it no more'—around and around and around. It wasn't a bad switching. It didn't leave any scars or anything. It was just to let us know not to do it again. And we didn't.''

She quickly moved to all the good things that Daddy had done—recreation, diversion. Earl believed that "the idle mind is the devil's workshop.'' She described how "my father wanted to know where we were at all times. Our friends were invited to our home any time. On Saturdays we could have our friends out to play tennis. We'd go swimming. Or we'd spend the night with someone so we could go to a midnight show. Mother and he went to Americus every Saturday night. He went to Americus, he said, because if he didn't buy a dozen glasses every Saturday night in Americus, he wouldn't have anything to drink out of on Sunday, because the kids broke the glasses.''

She described the nicknames Earl used toward the children. "Jimmy was called Junior Hotshot, and he always called me Go-go, which Jimmy also called me when I—from the time I was fourteen—and Ruth was called Boop-a-Doop.'' And she stressed the variant upbringing that Billy received. "Daddy said he tried to raise three of us right and we came out awful, so he was going to raise Billy just like he wanted to, and enjoy it. And he did. But Billy was right with Daddy all his life. He always had a little black playmate who was supposed to be looking after him, but Billy was such a little 'cotton trout'—blond child—and the playmate was just as black as you can imagine, and they used to ride on the back of Daddy's pick-up everywhere together. We called them Night and Day. The little boy is still one of Billy's best friends. He still sees him. But we always had our black playmates and we didn't know any different. Well, I guess we had black playmates until we went to school. Then we had young girls to come in and help with the housework. But we never considered them maids or anything.''

The conversation quickly led to A.D. Davis, Carter's closest childhood friend who was subsequently put in a chain-gang for manslaughter. Gloria said that when Jimmy was running for governor, a truckload of convicts came by and A.D. hollered from it: "Hey, Jimmy.'' Jimmy hollered back: "Hey, A.D.'' A.D. was subsequently paroled, not, according to Gloria, through Jimmy's influence, "but because it was a manslaughter charge.''

By now we had reached Billy's gas station and it was time to say goodbye. I was struck by the conditional way she did it, with much emphasis on my getting in touch with her if I had any other questions. In

Georgia, you are always urged to come back, to call, to promise to write, and everyone assures the departing guest that "they'll see you soon." Parting is denied. There is little overt acceptance of the notion that people can go their entirely separate ways.

A. D. DAVIS

Plains has a total residential population of 683, most of them are black, but on my first day in town I was hardly aware that blacks existed, so few of them were visible on the street. When I did find A. D. Davis at home, it seemed somehow symbolic that he had had an accident that day and his eyes were bandaged.

The interview was very productive, and began with A.D.'s rather idyllic vision of two boys hunting with their dogs and using their flips or slingshots—and, later, Earl's rifle—on the local small game. A.D. was a year or two younger than Jimmy, and dominated by him. In his own words, "Jimmy likes to star."

"I believe that he showed leader all the way," A.D. declared. "When he was a kid, he always loved to be—he always starred. He always liked to be the star. He was good at it. He was always wise. He looked like he wanted to amount to something. It seemed whatever we'd be doing, he'd be good at it—he'd make it good." And again: "He always had to be the head of it. He'd be the head." When they played baseball out in Archery, Jimmy had to be the pitcher.

But Jimmy matured late, and when he went off to college at the age of fifteen he was only 5'3". Still, his small stature did not affect his need to dominate—though he sometimes preferred reading books to playing.

A.D. was very positive about Lillian Carter, less so about Earl. "Miz Lillian, she's alright, she was nice, she was a nice lady. Mr. Earl, he was too, but he wasn't as nice as Miss Lillian was. Jimmy was more like his mom. And Billy was like his dad. He had ways with his mama, Jimmy did." A.D. pictured Lillian as something of a cross between Santa Claus and a protector. When he got a bloody nose in the course of wrestling with Jimmy, she would "whop" her son (Lillian is usually portrayed, incidentally, as never physically punishing her children). To quote A.D.: "I used to get Jimmy a heap of whoppings. That's what Miz Lillian gave to him. We'd do each other like that. I reckon that's the way a child does when he's coming up. I could beat him wrestling, but I couldn't beat him boxing. They had to give us boxing lessons—me, him, Rembert, and a crowd of us. My nose was easy to bleed, and that's it. A touch on my nose, I would see my blood and I would go tell Miz Lillian who'd whop him. And that would be my fault."

"What would Miss Lillian whop him with?" I asked. "She had a good old switching whop." And he added that Jimmy wasn't too much for fighting, which I could well understand.

Unliked the Carters, A.D. was convinced that Jimmy had been instrumental in getting his release from prison. He confirmed the fact that Ruth had been given a doll-like role in the family. And he confirmed Jimmy's own accuracy in details when he said that he himself had eleven children. "That's the first time I've heard of Jimmy being wrong," I commented. "He said you had fourteen kids." A.D. though about it for a while, then noted that if one counted the two who had died, and the one born out of wedlock when he was a "young colt," the correct figure was fourteen. His strong positive feelings about Jimmy seemed very real. "Jimmy was a good boy. He always was a good boy. He always wanted to do something for somebody else. He loved to help you out of tight spots." The fact that he tolerated the interview under conditions of severe anxiety and some pain was proof of his regard for Jimmy, and for the latter's desire to "help out."

ANNIE MAE JONES

When I drove up to her house, the first thing that impressed me about Annie Mae was her size: bigger than Lillian Carter, of course, but bigger than Earl too. She was very quiet and reserved—defensive—but helpful in most ways, and we talked for several hours, though I was surprised to learn that Jimmy was already six or seven when she came to help the Carters. (My assumption had been that she nursed him in early infancy.)

Annie Mae talked about the whoppings Earl had inflicted on Jimmy. She believed that Lillian did not whop Jimmy herself but simply said: "I'm going to tell your daddy about it." But her statements were cautious: "I never seen Miz Carter spank him. She never did. If she did, I never seen her." She spoke in detail about switching, but mainly from her own perspective as nurse and cleaning lady, and with much emphasis on how much worse her own switchings were: how her mother had made them raise their clothes above their heads, and had whipped them with several switches tied together, as opposed to Jimmy, who kept his clothes on and was beaten with only one switch at a time. She said that her mother made her thank her, made her say "Thank you, mama, for the good old whipping." I wondered if a woman who was beaten in this way could avoid being somewhat severe and embittered toward the children placed in her care.

Annie Mae stressed at some length the demanding quality of Lillian's function as a registered nurse. "Miz Lillian, she nursed day and night. She was just like a doctor. If anyone got sick on the place, she'd be right there." "I guess you had to take care of the kids," I noted. "I did. I did practically everything 'cause she would be on night duty. She'd leave in the evening and she wouldn't be back until the next morning. She'd come in and she'd have to go to bed and go to sleep. And be ready to go to work the next night. And I knew what to do. And I'd say, well, I'll stay with the children—cook, feed them. If they had to go to school, I'd get them off. I was right there every day. Sure was.''

Annie Mae also confirmed the favored status of Ruth. "Mr. Earl sure did love Ruth. He loved all his children, but you know, only 'cause she was the baby back then he let her have—I think whatever that baby wanted, she did, but probably 'cause she was the baby girl he loved her more. He loved all his children.''

Did Miss Lillian have a favorite? "Well, if she did I couldn't tell you. She'd treat one about the same as the others. I think she treated all of them about the same way. If she did [have a favorite], she didn't show it to me.''

There was a similarity between Lillian and Annie Mae when I mentioned Rosalynn. The same icy feelings emerged, but Annie Mae was less subtle as she crossed her arms, leaned back, and maintained that Teena Ratliff, rather than Ruth's friend Rosalynn, was the girl that Jimmy loved.

Annie Mae laughed with embarrassment when I asked about her use of the "boogie man" in controlling the Carter children. "Sometimes I'd get out there into playing, and I'd get tired, and I'd say: 'I'm gonna call the boogie man.' And they'd say: 'There ain't no boogie man.' And I'd say: 'I'm gonna call the boogie man,' and I'd go: 'Hush, hush now, the boogie man is coming.' All of them would get to crying and looking for the boogie man. They'd get scared. They'd get right around me. 'Annie Mae! Where is he?' Everyone being quiet while Annie Mae is looking for the boogie man. 'He'll be here! He's coming!' We played so much.''

Annie Mae spoke with concern of Willie Carter Spann—called "Toady"—the Carter nephew, son of Gloria, who is now in prison in California and who is a self-confessed bank-robber, dope addict, and homosexual. She particularly remembered the close relationship between Toady and Miss Lillian. "They were good to him. Whatever he wanted, they'd give it to him. He didn't have to suffer for anything. And his stepdaddy Walter was good to him, too.'' She tried to justify him as the victim of dope, and left the impression that she and Toady were also very close. She was particularly proud of the fact that the Carter children never called her "nigger.'' When they would get mad at her they would say: "I don't like you—you go home.'' And she would reply: "I ain't going nowhere. You goin' to mind me.'' Then, after a while, "they'd get all right and they'd come hug me. We'd hug one another and they'd be all right. We'd go out there and we'd play dolls and everything would be all right. But they never did call me anything but my name.''

PSYCHOANALYTIC REFLECTIONS ON JIMMY CARTER

In psychoanalytic terminology, Jimmy Carter can be considered a narcissistic personality with obsessive compulsive defenses. His narcissism is reflected in his need to gain praise to compensate for his own sense of inadequacy, stemming from insufficient emotional nurturance during early childhood. The psychoanalyst Otto Kernberg might very well have been writing about Carter when he said that narcissists "present an unusual degree of self reference in their interaction with other people, a great need to be loved and admired by others, and a curious apparent contradiction between a very inflated concept of themselves and an inordinate need of tribute from others."[1]

The oral rage characteristic of narcissistic personalities is reflected in different incidents in Jimmy Carter's childhood. While almost dying of colitis, at approximately 20 months, Jimmy screamed and screamed for a goat. Miss Abrams, Lillian's friend who was the Head Nurse at the Wise Sanitarium, went out and bought the first baby goat that she could find to pacify Jimmy.[2] It was kept in a little box by his bed. While keeping baby goats (kids) as pets is common in the rural South, I suspect that this 'kid' had special meaning to Jimmy. A goat is notoriously an oral-aggressive animal which will devour everything from clothes to tin cans in its insatiable need to bite. Having a "kid" of his own gave Jimmy his own "baby surrogate" to hold on to at a time when his mother was expecting the first of his three sibling rivals. The goat also may have served as a transitional object, a security blanket to compensate for the impending further loss of his mother's attention.

The issue of colitis is central to the understanding of Jimmy's fantastic drive for control.[3] He had lost control shortly after gaining it, and suffered great humiliation. The need for control that he experienced in the rest of his life reflects a genuine concern for controlling his own oral and anal rage. This rage was present in an incident recollected by his Aunt Sissy Dolvin, who was baby-sitting for young Jimmy when he bit through his pacifier. She said he screamed and yelled so vociferously that she had to walk to town and get the pharmacist to open up the store in order to get Jimmy another pacifier.[4] Jimmy Carter today masks his anger and rage with smiles. We have an unusual amount of material documenting this reaction formation, which probably began after the birth of his first baby sister.

Jimmy associated the birth of Gloria with punishment. He writes: "Most of my other punishments occurred because of arguments with my sister Gloria, who was younger than I, but larger, during our growing years. I remember once she threw a wrench and hit me, and I retaliated by shooting her in the rear end with a B.B. gun. For several hours, she reburst into tears every time the sound of a car was heard. When Daddy finally drove into our yard, she was apparently sobbing uncontrollably, and after a brief explanation by her of what had occurred, Daddy whipped me without further comment."[5] Gloria's birth resulted in the normal diminution of maternal attention, the presence of a rival who within several years was bigger than her older brother, and the open favorite of her father. That Earl nicknamed Gloria "Go-Go" was a further indication of the fact that she was an aggressive child, fighting for her share of what attention was paid the children in the Carter household. Jimmy reacted by being a bossy, controlling older brother. Since their father allowed no back talk and "sassing their mother" was the worst thing the Carter kids could do, Jimmy's rage had to go underground precisely when it became greatest.

At times Jimmy smiles when he'd prefer to bite. Cartoonists immediately recognized this and have been caricaturing this smile since he ran for Governor in 1966. They portray him as a smiling tiger or Cheshire Cat with a secret but never as an innocent kitten. It's his aggression and grandiosity that are portrayed. During the Presidential election, Jimmy's own staff was talking about Jimmy's "good smiles and his bad smiles." During the 27-minute "loss of audio" during the first Carter-Ford Presidential Debate in October of 1976, Jimmy continued to smile nervously while Ford frowned—but later Carter criticized his staff for letting him stand there feeling and appearing foolish with millions of television viewers watching.

While enduring the agony of first-year hazing at Annapolis, Jimmy wrote in his diary: "My problem is that I smile too much."[7] Because it constituted a reaction formation, he could define, but not overcome, this problem. When his smile became counterproductive, his aggression turned inward. Rather than suffer the humiliation of singing "Marching Through Georgia" and making endless speeches, Jimmy cut his gums and said that it was worth it. Another incident which reflects this reaction formation occurred while Jimmy was campaigning for governor. While hustling the crowds, Jimmy put his hand on the shoulder of a potential voter who proceeded to hit him harder than he had ever been hit before. While still nursing his bruised jaw, Jimmy wanted to apologize almost immediately upon learning that his assailant was a former mental patient recently back from Viet Nam. When Jimmy heard that the man involved had been reinstitutionalized at Milledgeville State Hospital, his first thought was to visit him to apologize personally. However, he was dissuaded from this and settled for a telephone call.

As is the case with other narcissistic personalities whose "emotional lives are shallow," Jimmy's interpersonal relations are generally superficial. He has contact with an extraordinary number of people but very little meaningful human interaction. The hallmark of Carter as a politician has been the *image* of intimacy. He has literally touched millions of people, which he confuses with actually getting to know them. To say "I love you" to factory workers on the 5:00 a.m. shift reveals what little depth he attaches to the concept of love. It is extraordinarily important to Jimmy to have this superficial contact with people because it is this "image of intimacy" with ordinary people and blacks which enables him to charge his psychic batteries and keep moving forward. Yet, the narcissistic triumph of having 9,000,000 people attempt to call him on a Saturday afternoon is short-lived because of this very shallowness.

Let us review Jimmy's interpersonal relations. His first recollection of his mother Lillian in his autobiography was that she was away helping others. When she was home she had her head in a book even at meals, a practice which he carries on. Although there were a number of black people who aided in the care of Jimmy Carter, there was apparently no one mother substitute with whom he could identify in the formative first six years. Furthermore, Lillian Carter's desire not to share her home with another woman is said by one witness to have led her to send black nannies like Annie Mae Jones away for several weeks at a time, thus interrupting Jimmy's own object relationships. Earl Carter was a concerned, rather intrusive father, who demanded very high standards of his firstborn son, while openly showing preference to the younger children. Jimmy's recollection of his father involved peach switchings, humiliations, entrepreneurial skill, and competence—qualities which placed his father above criticism.[9] The evidence of internal poverty of object relations explains why Jimmy gives the impression of growing up poor while his siblings and neighbors refer to the Carter family as having been quite well-off.

Growing up as a white Southern boy in a densely populated black neighborhood meant that Jimmy had to learn to combine distance and intimacy along racial lines. In childhood, blacks were the common people to Jimmy, and they took on a special meaning as representatives of his repressed desires. Earl Carter facilitated this process by coupling each of his children with a black helper/playmate. It is interesting to note that Gloria said Billy's little black playmate "was supposed to be looking after him." In school, Jimmy, who was undersized and very late in maturing, was taught to relate to people through academic and sport competitions. At Annapolis, after a year of intense hazing, Jimmy related to his peers essentially by helping them with their studies. That he chose his wife from among his sister's girlfriends is indicative of the shyness of which he himself has spoken. His marriage to Rosalynn has been characterized by a large number of separations. His decision to become an officer in a submarine virtually insured long absences from her and the children. After a disagreement with his father about race,

Jimmy barely returned at all to Plains to see his family for eleven years. Being an officer in the submarine corps offered an "intimate distance," since he was physically very close to others yet emotionally very contained and controlled.

To quote Jimmy: "Admiral Rickover had a profound effect on my life—perhaps more than anyone except my own parents.[10] His unconscious motivation for choosing this man as his adult model was that, like his father, Rickover was demanding and denigrating. The only reward he could expect for a job well done was a lack of criticism. Now that, as President, he is Rickover's commander-in-chief, and has recently been praised by his idol, one wonders what shifts of roles will now take place. There is already the evidence of the way he has handled his energy program to show that he is assuming the position of the punitive father. The danger, of course, is that this role of punitive father to the nation will be the main source of his actions as President, to the exclusion of the human warmth and feeling which more rarely comes across in his personality. The ambivalence and distancing which I felt so strongly in my interview with his mother, and which were the emotional reality of Jimmy Carter's early years, will undoubtedly prove to have a strong influence on the future of the country he now leads.[10]

Paul H. Elovitz, Ph.D. is an Assistant Professor of History and Politics at Ramapo College, Mahwah, New Jersey, where he teaches psychohistory and related courses. He is a Contributing Editor to The Journal of Psychohistory *and a Research Associate at The Institute for Psychohistory. He is also a psychotherapist in private practice in Teaneck and Oakland, New Jersey, a candidate at the New Jersey Institute for Training in Psychoanalysis, and is completing a book-length study of Jimmy Carter.*

REFERENCES

1. Kernberg, Otto, *Borderline Conditions and Pathological Narcissism,* New York: Jason Aronson, Inc. 1973, p. 227. The obsessive defenses will be explored elsewhere.
2. Telephone interviews with Miss Abrams.
3. See Sperling, Melita, "Psychoanalytic Study of Ulcerative Colitis in Children," *Psychoanalytic Quarterly* XV (1946), pp. 302-329.
4. Telephone interview with Emily (Cissy) Dolvin.
5. Carter, Jimmy, *Why Not The Best,* New York: Bantam Books, 1975, p. 12.
6. Interviews with both Gloria and Lillian Carter on October 27, 1976.
7. *Annapolis Diary.* In the possession of Lillian Carter, Unpaginated.
8. Kernberg, *op. cit.,* p. 227.
9. Carter, *op. cit.,* p. 13.
10. *Ibid.,* pp. 8-19.

CHAPTER THREE

Toward a Psychohistory of Jimmy Carter

DAVID R.
BEISEL

THE CARTER FAMILY IN GROUP-FANTASY

Long ago, America created an elaborate mythology around the office
of the Presidency. Contemporary America has already added to that
earlier mythology by erecting an elaborate new myth around Jimmy
Carter. Part of the process has been of Carter's own design. The autobiographical words of *Why Not the Best?,* the elaborate media
manipulations of the campaign and after, and the policies articulated
and pursued by the Carter Administration are and were calculated to
build the kind of image that would win for him in November, 1976, and
presumably will win again in 1980. Yet myth formation works in two
ways. While Carter has conveyed to us the image of the kind of leader he
thinks we want, in various ways we have conveyed to him the kind of
leader we think we want him to be. As Presidential candidate, as President-elect, and finally as President, Carter has been, and remains, a
highly receptive receptacle for what Lloyd deMause has termed our
historical "group-fantasies."[1]
One way in which the individual leader can interact with the group is
through a merger of the individual's fantasy with the national group-
fantasy. A preponderant theme is Carter's own self-image—one which
resonates perfectly with the contemporary American group-fantasy—
was revealed by a *New York Daily News* headline on the day following

Carter's inauguration as thirty-ninth President of the United States. The headline celebrated two events: the unprecedented mile-and-a-half walk from the Capitol to the White House during the "People's Inaugural," and the earlier come-from-nowhere presidential victory on November 2. The *Daily News* called both events "A Long March by a Family United."[2] Family is the operative word. As much as Jimmy himself, it has been all the Carters who have fascinated America. In mid-February, columnist Harriet van Horne commented: "Wherever you go these days, people are talking about the Carters. In less than a month, the new First Family has made an indelible mark on the public psyche and the world press." Indeed, Ms. van Horne was herself beguiled. After briefly quoting a satirical jibe at Carter and his mother, Miss Lillian, by the British humor magazine *Punch,* van Horne concluded protectively: "Let the word go forth from these wild shores. If any fun is to be poked at our president, we'll do the poking."[3]

All along we have been and continue to be fascinated with the President's relatives, his sons, his daughters-in-law, his grandchildren, with his sisters, Gloria Carter Spann and evangelist Ruth Carter Stapleton, and with the President's younger brother, who, as a new folk hero, has even called forth a book, *Redneck Power: The Wit and Wisdom of Billy Carter.*[4]

America's common concern with the Carters has been neither temporate nor transitory. We have begun to idealize and glorify them. "The Carters are an unusually close family," wrote Charlotte Curtis in *McCall's.* "They are their own best friends and advisors and always have been. There's nothing any of them like more than getting together." Late-night television talk-show host Johnny Carson, whose powerful influence on America is shown in his 1974 joke creating a scarcity of toilet tissue, notified America in January 1977 that the President's mother, Miss Lillian, "is delightful, like everyone's grandmother." Long before, America's women's magazines had decided that Jimmy and Rosalynn were the perfect couple, the perfect parents, while nine-year-old daughter Amy, embracing her dog Grits on *Time*'s cover, seems to be taking on the characteristics of the perfect child. In an interview with a Delegate from Abroad to the Democratic National Convention, the Delegate's wife, a social worker, spontaneously told me that, "As a model for America, it's going to be wonderful to have an extended family back home in the White House again."[5]

It may be that our idealization of the Carters is part of a pattern that is absolutely essential to us in all our First Families. But I do not remember such intense national preoccupation with the families of Richard Nixon or Gerald Ford. Part of the reason for our first fascination with the Carters stems from the realities of their national obscurity: we are curious and simply want to know more about them. Another reason stems from

Carter's continuous, seemingly compensatory, comments that his family is vitally important to him, a theme repeated in almost every Carter speech and interview during the campaign and after and reiterated by other Carters. Yet these private reasons merely feed a group-fantasy function for our fascination with them as a model family, one stemming in part from the present precarious position of the modern American family. Divorce is on the rise, and, from numerous other sources in our society, our families seem somehow endangered. Public preoccupations with the American family reveal an uneasiness about the long-term security of our basic institution of nurturance and intimacy. It is an uneasiness which has recently taken the form of what historian Edward Shorter has called "the marriage and the family business."[6] The proliferation of new sociology courses, the creation of new scholarly journals, even Shorter's own book are part of it. By mythologizing the Carters and turning them into the perfect family, we are at least in part defending against anxieties created by the uncertainties of our own families' futures. Vicarious belonging, fantasies of mutual support, and a sense of illusory security are the possible rewards of identification with the First Family's presumed perfection.

Yet we know perfectly well that even in the most "normal" families perfection does not prevail. Structural family therapist Salvador Minuchin notes that in America, despite "sociological and anthropological studies of the family, the myth of placid normality endures, supported by hours of two-dimensional television characters. The picture of people living in harmony, coping with social inputs without getting ruffled, and always cooperating with each other, crumbles whenever one looks at any family with its ordinary problems."[7] In developing a Carter psychohistory, we should expect to find stress and tension within the Carter matrix. The question is not whether stress and tension exist, but how much, how they are handled, and what is made of them by American group-fantasy. Corollary questions include how family dynamics might relate to the November 2 presidential victory and what these dynamics might mean for the conduct of the Carter presidency.

For answers to these questions, the psychohistorian must try to assess the major formative influences on Carter in his major formative period, his childhood. We cannot attempt here a comprehensive reconstruction of Carter's early years since our evidence grows with each day, and since the issues are too complex, far-reaching and multifaceted for a single essay. What we can do is point to one central element in Carter's upbringing, an element that at this early stage of research appears crucial, since Carter seems to have been attempting to deal with it, and has kept repeating it, throughout much of his adult life. It lies in his relationship with his mother.

As we turn to the evidence for Carter's childhood, we should expect it

to have been already distorted by the group-fantasy of family perfection. Political psychologist James David Barber summarized current
opinion in *Time*'s "Man of the Year" issue when he said that bits "of
evidence from his early times confirm Carter's memories of love and
challenge, of parents who were 'there' in fact."[8] A more realistic appraisal,
but one still affected by the group-fantasy, was offered by Bruce Mazlish
and Edwin Diamond in the first published psychohistorical article on
Carter. "As for how his parents raised him," they wrote, "what counts
most is what Jimmy remembers. In Carter's memories, the father looms
largest. And contrary to current notions that Lillian, the mother, was the
major formative influence, we believe the father to have been at least as,
and probably, more significant."[9] So far the evidence uncovered on
Carter's father (which we cannot go into here) seems to indicate that he
was indeed important—particularly later in Jimmy's life. In Mazlish and
Diamond's words, "Carter's father can be seen as caring." Obviously,
the surface picture of James Earl Carter, Sr., as an "unfeeling, conservative disciplinarian" is too pat. On the other hand, the evidence demon-
strates that, contrary to what Mazlish and Diamond argue, Jimmy's
mother, not his father, was indeed the major formative influence in his
life—but not in the way most have believed.

Mazlish and Diamond's piece points out (and it is a basic assumption of almost all biographers) that Carter's attitude toward his mother is
undoubtedly ambivalent: "She never whipped him, though she spanked
him . . . [but] she, as a nurse, was clearly the nurturant, caring figure."[10]
Doubtless, Miss Lillian does care a great deal about her oldest son—and
the rest of her children—but the Mazlish-Diamond argument is based on
scanty evidence. In fact, the logic of their basic assumption, that *because*
she was a nurse she was nurturant and caring, is faulty. The logic of
nurse-nurturance, in itself, is not persuasive (as if no one enters nursing
for reasons other than healing). For a clearer understanding of the
mother-son interactions of Jimmy Carter's childhood and adult life, we
must look more closely at the evidence.

LILLIAN CARTER AS MOTHER

Obviously, Lillian Carter is no ordinary woman. In some senses she
has become America's idol, as—symbolic of her popularity—large numbers of autograph seekers (reaching, by her own reckoning, 1,800 one
Sunday) daily lined the streets of Plains during and after the presidential
campaign patiently awaiting her autograph. Wanting her to conform to
their maternal ideal, people often related to her out of their own experiences: often, in her words, "somebody wants to tell me about the history
of their mother's life."[11] She has been in demand by the media, giving

numerous interviews to women's and news magazines and to electronic journalists. In these interviews she projects the image of a vigorous, outspoken, opinionated woman whose energy belies her seventy-eight years.

In his public statements and actions concerning his mother, Carter seems on the surface to relate to Miss Lillian in conventional ways. His behavior serves to reinforce the group-fantasy as he consistently reiterates how much he admires and respects her. Unlike his statements about his father (primarily in his autobiography), we detect few hints of criticism or hostility directed toward her. So uncritical and persistently positive are his comments that (political considerations aside) we begin to suspect the possibility of a reaction formation. It will be one of the main themes of this paper that Jimmy does not view Miss Lillian realistically, as a woman with faults as well as virtues, but has turned whatever anger he feels towards her into a fantasy vision of the perfect mother.

We may begin to detect some of Jimmy's repressed anger toward Miss Lillian in the fact that his autobiography devotes less space to her than to his father. Of course, one possible explanation for this might be that he feels his father was a more formative influence in his life and hence spent more time on Earl. Another explanation might be that by giving Lillian less space in *Why Not the Best?* Jimmy is avoiding dredging up painful childhood memories.

We can, however, begin to detect some of Jimmy's true feelings toward his mother with the autobiography itself. During Jimmy's childhood and adolescence, Lillian Carter worked as a nurse. Jimmy tells us that "during my formative years, she worked constantly, primarily on private duty either at the nearby hospital or in patients' homes. She typically worked on nursing duty twelve hours per day, or twenty hours per day, for which she was paid the magnificent sum of six dollars," or, quite often, nothing. She also "served as a community doctor for our neighbors and for us and was extremely compassionate towards all those who were afflicted with any sort of illness."[12] In addition to being absent from the home much of the time (the phrase "twelve hours . . . or twenty hours" seems almost childlike, a shorthand for a long, long time), it appears that Miss Lillian also tended to be withdrawn when she was with the family. According to Peter Goldman's *Newsweek* account, "her children when they saw her at all between her nursing rounds remember her buried in books even at table during meals."[13] In a radio interview, Carter's sister, Ruth Carter Stapleton, confirms the pattern of maternal inaccessability, remembering that "each of us had a . . . a nurse when we grew up and then we had one . . . ah, young person assigned to us a couple of years older to take care of us step by step."[14] The hesitations in Ruth Stapleton's otherwise flowing speech (which come before remembrances of mother-substitutes) reveal some of her repressed anger. Miss Lillian's modest involvement with Jimmy's upbringing is reconfirmed by ninety-year-old Miss Rachel Clark. Asked by interviewers from the children's magazine, *Children's Express,* how long she had worked for the Carters, Jimmy's black-nanny replied: "It was fifty-some years. It was when the children were small. I helped raise them children, four of them," a fact Miss Lillian repeated in her own *Children's Express* interview. It is important that the eleven-year-old *Children's Express* interviewer understood Miss Clark's statement that she "helped raise them children" to be the equivalent of "She brought up Jimmy Carter." Further indications from the research of psychohistorian Paul Elovitz make it appear that there is another, earlier, perhaps more important black-nanny in Carter's childhood. It may be a significant symptom of denial that Carter never mentions either of them in his autobiography. Hopefully, future research will uncover the quality and meaning of these relationships.[15]

The kind of treatment the Carter children received from Miss Lillian may have been interpreted by the child Jimmy in the same sense that his sister Ruth understood it. "My mother didn't indulge me as my father did," she writes in her book, *The Gift of Inner Healing.* "She treated all the children alike. This registered on my emotions as rejection."[16] Yet from the pages of Carter's autobiographical account (the book is dedicated to Lillian and Rosalynn) there emerges a different, more glowing picture of his mother. She is portrayed in almost totally idealized form as a concerned, hard-working woman who obtained great satisfaction from helping others. This is Carter's conscious image, the one he wants us to share.

There is undoubtedly a good deal of truth to it. As Glenn Davis' fine study, *Childhood and History in America* has suggested about general patterns, and from other evidence relating specifically to Lillian's style of parenting, she seems to have been among the most advanced types of mothers in the 1920's.[17] According to Mazlish and Diamond, she breast-fed Jimmy for six months and devoted herself to treating two-year-old Jimmy's severe case of colitis from which many children died in the period. Nor did she leave the family setting for years on end or send her children away to live with others for extended periods, as did Hannah Nixon.[18] Lillian Carter was not a "bad" mother. Yet we sense tendencies in her to remove herself from intimate family surroundings for short periods and notice her efforts to achieve isolation at home. With all her activity, with the care of the children given over to others, we wonder about the extent of her involvement with her own children. What kind of time remained for Jimmy and his siblings, particularly when, for the limited hours they were together, she often distanced herself emotionally from them by reading at the dinner table?

It does not seem that such behavior supports Barber's contention that Carter enjoyed the advantages of "parents who were 'there' in fact."

The reverse seems true. It is not unusual for the children of mothers like Miss Lillian to perceive such "distancing" parenting as rejection. It is not difficult to reconstruct a quite different scenario from Barber's of Carter's childhood. An isolated Jimmy had to share his mother's limited affection with his oldest sister Gloria, two years his younger. (While his mother was nearing term in her pregnancy with Gloria, two-year-old Jimmy suffered the colitis from which he nearly died and noted in his autobiography: "Most of my punishments occurred because of arguments with my sister Gloria.")[19]

Later, at the crucial age of five, the lonely Jimmy was forced to share his mother's and his nanny's affections with another sister, Ruth. Throughout this period, Jimmy knew that his mother would be away from the family for long hours caring for others and not for him, knew that she would be close to home—"at the nearby hospital"—but not in the home, and knew that when she did return, tired from long hours of labor, she would seek refuge from family intimacy in books. An affection-starved Jimmy could not obtain all the love he needed from a demanding father and, in his words, a "stern disciplinarian" who began "switching" him, in Jimmy's adult recollection, at age four.

Jimmy had no other recourse but to try to obtain his mother's affection by becoming like her. "Although my father seldom read a book," he tells us, "my mother was an avid reader and so was I." But reading apparently failed to win her attention and Carter sought solace from surrogate-mother Rachel Clark. "He liked to do work," she said, "he loved to just follow me to work. He liked to pick cotton. He liked to go fishing all day. He would go with me fishin'—we'd stay all day. He followed me around and he followed my husband." Carter also sought solace from mother-substitute "Sissy" Dolvin, his mother's younger sister and his favorite aunt, who at one point refused to join a family picnic and, taking pity on, in her words, the "little and forlorn" seven-year-old Jimmy, stayed behind with him in the fields after he had been left there by the family as punishment for not pruning a watermelon patch. Carter also sought solace from another mother substitute, spinster school-superintendent Miss Julia Coleman whom, he claims, "heavily influenced my life." Having internalized his mother's propensity for reading, it was for mother-substitute Coleman that Carter, age twelve, read the 1400 pages of *War and Peace,* a work which "turned out to be one of my favorite books." Miss Coleman must have provided Carter with some of the maternal attention he felt lacking in his home. Later, he would recall how Miss Coleman rewarded his dedication to books: "She would give me a gold star when I read ten and a silver star when I read five."[20] Of the almost infinite number of people Carter could have chosen to cite, Miss Julia Coleman was the only person Carter quoted and mentioned by name in his Inaugural Address.

Miss Lillian's attitude toward and treatment of her son have not changed much since his childhood. That she continues to maintain her distance from Jimmy is suggested by events surrounding Carter's Inauguration. One of the most spirited performances presented to the Carter family in the Inaugural Eve Concert at Washington's Kennedy Center came from Mike Nichols and Elaine May. After being introduced by actor Jack Nicholson with the words, "Twenty years ago Mike Nichols and Elaine May burst upon the national scene with the sharp irreverence that started us laughing at our most treasured national neuroses," the "neurosis" they chose to share with us once again was their famous mother-son interchange over the telephone, this time built around a future, first Jewish president (with Carter cast in the role of "my-son-the-president"). The premise of the routine was that a too-busy son has failed to telephone his mother and his oversight is making her ill. The exchange makes open use of great maternal hostility directed toward the son as May utilizes the techniques of reverse statement, denial and understatement to instill guilt. At the end of their conversation she has triumphed by figuratively beating her son into submission and takes on the voice of the mother of a two- or three-year-old. Mostly through voice rhythms and modulations, Nichols has regressed to earlier and earlier stages of childhood concluding with: "Bye, bye mommy. Nanny nu . . . nanny nunny." President-elect Carter and Rosalynn were laughing cheerfully, but from the brief glimpses the television cameras gave us of Miss Lillian's passive face it did not appear that she particularly enjoyed the routine. Perhaps Nichols and May reflected too many of the underlying realities in her own mother-son relationship. As it was, on the next day, as President Carter's Inaugural Address came to a close, she remained seated and, according to the *New York Daily News,* [21] did not applaud.

We recall Ruth Carter Stapleton's statement that Miss Lillian "treated all the children alike." We should then expect Miss Lillian's attitudes and behavior toward the President's younger brother Billy to parallel those in her relationship with Jimmy. They seem to. Asked by Dan Rather about Billy's beer drinking she replied: "Dan . . . ah . . . I have never . . . in my life, said anything to Jimmy 'bout Billy, 'bout his drinkin'. I have never. And I have seen him, you know, when he's had a few. But I never have. I don't believe in naggin'." Expressions of maternal concern seem to be construed by Miss Lillian as nagging. The consequent distancing between her and her youngest son appear to be reciprocated. Dan Rather asked Billy if, because of the flood of strangers into Plains, he was concerned with his mother's safety. Billy replied: "Well . . . she will do what she wants to anyway—so there's nothing really, they, uh, uh, they, uh, look after her pretty good over there anyway." [22] It does not appear that Billy Carter is entirely happy with his mother's, and his own perhaps feigned unconcern. The fact is that the crowds in Plains do jostle and push Miss Lillian and she has been made black and blue by unwanted embraces. Billy, perhaps accepting the inevitable, has subsequently moved away.

Objectively, Miss Lillian may have treated all her children alike but she has frequently singled out one or another of her children—never Jimmy—as her favorite as, for example, in her comment that "Jimmy says that I've always loved Billy the best. Maybe I did." More often she has declared that "Gloria is my favorite." In view of Jimmy's perception of Gloria as the major sibling rival of his childhood, such statements by his mother must have intensified his sense of rejection. This open statement of preference has continued. Miss Lillian's current "favorite" is the President's nine-year-old daughter, Amy. During the campaign the seventy-eight-year-old grandmother said, "I have a very important part in the campaign. I'm taking care of Amy." She felt it necessary to say that "Jimmy's being president won't affect my life a whole lot, I don't suspect, except that it'll break my heart for Amy to go away from me. She's my heart, you know—I love her better than Jimmy." In a post-election interview she expressed the same sentiments. In response to a question about how she will feel when everyone leaves Plains and goes off to Washington, she said, "I'm going to miss Amy, but I won't miss Jimmy."[23]

Some have dismissed such statements as natural, as the common attitudes of American grandparents who "always tend to love their grandchildren more than their own children." This may be true—and creates another research problem for the psychohistorian. But more often than attempting to explain such statements, observers have responded to the real content of Miss Lillian's words about her son with total denial. The real meaning of the words do not fit the current group-fantasy. Novelist Raynolds Price judged that "you may gather Miss Lillian has all but exhausted her desire to reminisce about Jimmy now . . . She hasn't though. She adores him." This is what Price, and America, want to believe—that she adores him. More perceptive may be the insight of the twelve-year-old *Children's Express* reporter: "I was really surprised when we asked her [Miss Lillian] about the issues—she said 'Oh, I don't know about the issues. . .'—and she seemed like such a smart person up to that point. I was really surprised that she didn't know what her son stood for." Nor did Miss Lillian play the prideful mother during the campaign. When asked about Jimmy's childhood she invariably answered in stock phrases how ordinary he was. "There was nothing outstanding about Jimmy at all. He made good grades, but so did the rest of the children. There was nothing special about Jimmy." Such judgments stand in stark contrast to those of others, like Carter's eighty-eight-year-old uncle Alton, who praised his nephew by remembering that Jimmy "was just tip-tops every way. All his life."[24] Indeed, many of Miss Lillian's statements suggest that she learned as much about Jimmy's real feelings from reading his autobiography as from her own experiences.

Another bit of evidence suggestive of Miss Lillian's attitude toward Jimmy, and further confirmation of her mothering style, comes to us from two unexpected, but not unrelated sources: her treatment of her son's childhood memorabilia, and her treatment of male interviewers interested in Jimmy's boyhood. Lillian Carter dismisses as superficial anyone interested in her son's early life. She told Mike Douglas that after the election a Russian came by to interview her and she "took care of him: he was only interested in Jimmy as a boy." It is probable that she "took care" of the Russian journalist in much the same way that she "took care" of journalist William Greider. When he inquired about materials from Jimmy's childhood, "Mrs. Carter," Greider reports, "did not exactly dote over the material—she handed a stack of old school papers to the visitor and promptly left the house to run errands." Exactly the same behavior has been reported by psychohistorian Paul Elovitz during his interview with Miss Lillian in the last days of the presidential campaign. After presenting him with apparently the same childhood materials she revealed to Greider, Elovitz reports, "she left me alone in the house for about an hour to run errands."[25]

We might have expected a prideful mother to linger longer over the products of her famous son's childhood, especially if those reviewing the materials are genuinely interested. Instead Miss Lillian "laid out the goodies" and left. It is curious behavior for a woman who has expressed angry dismay at "all the dirt they're dredging up about these people" (the Kennedys and Nixons). Her disinterest in Jimmy's childhood memorabilia suggests a rejection of Jimmy's childhood. By abandoning the interviewers, Miss Lillian symbolically abandoned her son and virtually recreated her own mothering style with Jimmy as a child.

This behavior is not unexpected since Miss Lillian has been recreating the flight-from-home pattern throughout much of her adult life. She tells us in an interview that after the death of Earl in 1953, which left her "bitter . . . because everyone had a husband and I didn't," she "became a fraternity house-mother at Auburn University"[26] in Auburn, Alabama, approximately seventy-five miles from Plains. Miss Lillian has linked her move to Auburn to the death of her husband. It may have been partly inspired, on the unconscious level, by Jimmy's resignation from the Navy and his return, after an eleven-year absence, with his wife and children to Plains. While we will want to know the precise monthly chronology of Earl's death, Jimmy's return and Lillian's move, it may have been that Jimmy's arrival, and his arrival with children, sparked her to recreate her earlier role as a distancing mother in not-so-disguised form as she became a "mother" for others at an Auburn fraternity house.

There she remained for some time. In the same interview, Miss Lillian goes on to tell us that, "After seven and a half years I came back to Plains and managed a nursing home for a year and a half." Then, at age 67, inspired by a television commercial for the Peace Corps ("Age Is No Barrier"), she subsequently went off to treat lepers in India. Again in evidence are Miss Lillian's spunk, spontaneity and remarkable energies; also evident is the repeated pattern of distancing the family, where ambivalent feelings are intensified, fleeing to the outside world where she could continue to treat largely anonymous (and less threatening) strangers in order to assuage some of the guilt for not dealing more intimately with her own family.

Yet Miss Lillian has managed to successfully rationalize her role as an emotionally distancing parent. "I do believe in working women," she said in a *Ms. Magazine* interview, "and I feel so strongly that a child is better off not to have the mother every minute of the time. Children who cling to their mothers—they grow up being babies. And I think it's good for a mother and a child to be separated most of the day."[27]

Her family has come to expect it. When she announced her decision to join the Peace Corps, Jimmy reports, "We were not particularly surprised."[28] Yet significantly, Lillian had made her momentous Peace Corps decision in 1966 on impulse from a television commercial while Jimmy was running for governor. Whether she was emotionally unable to handle the possibility of her son's defeat, or whether it was an inability to handle the possibility of her son's victory (which would have meant that Jimmy had achieved success beyond her husband's), Miss Lillian was leaving home again. It is this dramatic renewal of the old distancing pattern, not the loss of the Georgia governorship alone, which should probably be linked to Carter's now famous pre-"born again" depression of 1966 since we know that "conversion" experiences are manic solutions to deep depressive episodes set off by emotional crises, often an emotional abandonment, real or imagined.[29] And, as we shall see, both of Jimmy's sisters, having difficulties within their own families, underwent similar conversion experiences.

It seems to have been exceedingly difficult for Lillian Carter to have been able to enjoy any kind of meaningful family intimacy throughout her life, although she has apparently wanted to. In what seems a defensive reaction, she has said: "I never cared much about my kin. I'll tell you why. We were the poor side of the family, and they didn't know me till Jimmy was governor."[30] She obviously did care—or would not have mentioned it. Poverty can sometimes be used as rationalization for the act of distancing members of a family, but the behavior, and its consequences, remains the same—and, in any case, the Carters who owned a farm, employed farm labor and domestic servants, and ran a general store, were not really impoverished. Rejection seems to run as a persistent thread throughout the Carters' family history.

THE PARENTING STYLES OF RUTH, GLORIA, AND JIMMY

Miss Lillian's overall distancing of her children has contributed to a family transactional pattern among the Carters known to structural family therapists as disengagement. "The clarity of boundaries within a family," writes Salvador Minuchin, "is a useful parameter for the evaluation of family functioning." Some families turn inward, creating a microcosm in which concern and communication increase to a point where articulated and unexpressed boundaries between individuals tend to disappear, creating in extreme situations the polarity of enmeshment. Other families, like the Carters, create greatly differentiated boundaries in which communication and emotional involvement are increasingly difficult, the polarity of disengagement. Most families fall into the middle range on the continuum between these two extremes, but the disengagement-enmeshment polarities should be understood to be preferential styles, not functional-dysfunctional modes. "Operations at the extremes, however, indicate areas of possible pathology," writes Minuchin. "Members of disengaged subsystems . . . may function autonomously but have a skewed sense of independence and lack feelings of loyalty and belonging and capacity for interdependence and for requesting support when needed."[31]

It has been demonstrated many times over how we tend to recreate as adults the transactional patterns of our childhoods. Disengagement and fear of intimacy, both partly learned from Miss Lillian, have been faithfully recreated in part by her children in their own families. An example of this kind of intergenerational transmission, and the best evidence for it, comes from the experiences of Ruth Carter Stapleton.

In the first years of her marriage, Ruth had difficulties in relating to her children. As she writes in *The Gift of Inner Healing*:[32]

> A major crisis arose when I discovered I was pregnant with my first child. I knew that this was supposed to be one of the crowning moments of womanhood, but not for me. No one knew how I trembled inside. I was not prepared to deal with such responsibilities. When my baby was born, I wanted to be a good mother, but I felt even more trapped. I felt like such a failure. Bottles and diapers were hard enough. I knew the care and comfort my baby needed, but I felt as much need for this as that darling baby I was sometimes afraid to hold. Then three more babies were born in rapid succession, and each one, so beautiful, terrified me.

Ruth Carter Stapleton had never satisfactorily internalized a maternal image, perhaps because the one she had of Miss Lillian was vague and indistinct. Intimacy was extremely difficult. She could not cuddle with the children whom she both loved and feared. "I have never been able to cope with little babies very well," she said in a radio interview. Flowing from this, and brought on and intensified by becoming a mother four times over, was deep depression. It was a corollary to her mothering and apparently lasted for some time. Eventually the events at a week-long prayer retreat, where she had sought escape from her psychological pain, brought her a glimmer of hope. She was able to vent her anger and anxieties by unloading to a friendly psychologist ("I could do it with a stranger whereas I had never been able to share any part of my life before"). In the process she discovered the healing qualities of unconditional love. She came to the conviction, perhaps not at that moment, that if the psychologist loved her, "and he's only human, how much greater would God's love be?" She found in Jesus what had been missing from her family and childhood settings—unconditional love. She argues today that if individuals find it difficult to give or receive love, "it's probably because you didn't receive adequate love from a mother-father relationship."[33]

The "inner healings" Ruth Carter Stapleton now performs for others recreate in some measure the non-involved intimacy with strangers of her mother's nursing days. Her personal breakthrough and new life task, however, do not seem to have improved relationships within the disengaged Carter system. Had she "healed" Jimmy Carter? "Oh, no . . . Oh, no. I've never . . . I've never . . . done any work with any of my family. I think that's natural, you know. I think your . . . your family would be the last to ask you to, and they would be the last one's I'd want to." The hesitations in her speech again reflect tensions which this time may reveal that part of her still very much wants to "work" with her family and that displaced evangelical involvements with strangers as family substitutes are not satisfying enough. For within the Carter context, personal disengagements seem as strong as ever. Was Jimmy made uncomfortable by her religious work during the campaign? "I didn't think he knows an awful lot about my work and my ministry. I think it was a little bit of a shock for him to know I was connected in healing. I don't think he knew that before the press . . . you know, started writing articles."[34] Carter has said that he has not seen much of Ruth over the past several years, yet his sister's perception of his uncaring attitude seems a strange admission in a family supposedly close-knit and mutually supportive.

Besides disengagement, individual members of the Carter family have recapitulated their childhood experiences in their own families in other ways. Their life patterns confirm what appear to be the distancing parent and flight-from-home models provided by Miss Lillian. We should expect this to be especially true for Carter's sisters, Gloria and Ruth, since, as women, they would have been most likely to internalize whatever bits and pieces of a maternal model they could gather from Miss Lillian.

Troubled by the difficulties encountered in dealing with a rebellious son, and convinced like Ruth before her, that she was "a complete failure as a mother," Gloria Carter Spann found release, as other Carters have, by turning to God. In the early 1960s she began attending prayer retreats "at least twice a year, sometimes more. I told my husband that I had to repay God for His grace to me. I loved the retreats; I enjoyed my weekly prayer group and I volunteered for any job anywhere that would ease someone else's load." As her mother, and as sister Ruth and brother Jimmy, Gloria justified her absences from her household by her aid to anonymous strangers. Her husband, Walter Spann, "remained at home, trying to live as normal a life with his friends, having fun and laughing, as we used to do together. He never complained about my absences; silently he endured my fanaticism. He was probably glad to see me go off."

The pattern lasted for some time, until in 1969, Gloria attended her last prayer retreat. "It was glorious . . . but something was happening inside me, something I felt was *wrong.*" Unable to fully understand her uneasiness, she isolated herself in the retreat's prayer room and confessed to God that she was even willing to give up her husband for Him. Suddenly she heard the words: "How about giving up prayer retreats?" What troubled her was guilt derived from the reality that her pursuit of religion amounted to the abandonment of her husband. "I realized it would truly be an act of God to be able to stay home." But she was uncertain whether she would be able to change her life style. "Could it work? Could I reinforce my beliefs without the brace of a retreat? Could I live a completely routine life, be a happy housewife. . .?" She began to think more and more of her husband: "For the first time I was homesick, *really* homesick." Although she may not have been fully aware of it, Gloria Carter Spann had shattered the constraints of her mother's model and was now able to break through to that part of herself that really mattered. She found, in the love of her own home, the meaning of her life. "I had searched and searched for a reason for living and now I had one."[35]

In its essentials, Ruth Carter Stapleton's life tells a similar story. Deeply depressed by her inabilities to cope with being a wife and a mother, her first inclination was "to take the next slow boat to China and never come back." Instead she sought help and new direction from a prayer retreat. At the time, "my husband was at home taking care of the four children." Like many others she faced adversity by flight: "I was accustomed to removing myself from situations if they were unpleasant." In itself, this behavior is not unusual. In the context of the Carter family it is almost the only expected response. Today Ruth Carter Stapleton has visited "all the continents." In her own reckoning, her evangelical mission keeps her on lecture tour "at least 50 percent of the time." Service and hard work have justified her actions for, "If I didn't see lives changed . . . there are many things I could do at home—rest, play, enjoy myself, 'cause this is a very hard life to travel like this." She has recreated the maternal image of her mother as nurse in her own childhood through her religious healings, and rationalized it by saying: "It would have to be something, I think, so big as this for me to leave my family."[36]

From these hints about the dynamics of the Carter family, there emerge the themes of disengagement, flight-from-home, and distanced parenting which shed light on Miss Lillian's maternal style and her relationships with Jimmy. They are also themes which have been recreated by Carter in his own life both as parent and as husband.

In his late-adolescent and early-adult life, from Annapolis until the end of his eleven-year naval career, Jimmy Carter returned to visit his mother and father in Plains only briefly and on rare occasions. It is a pattern indicative of disengagement, of negative feelings about family, and of the model of family avoidance learned in childhood. It was a pattern justified, and guaranteed, by the choice of a naval career. It was a pattern imposed on his wife and family.

While Jimmy Carter was away on extended ocean cruises, Rosalynn Smith Carter, whom he had married upon graduating from Annapolis, was left behind in Norfolk, in Oahu, in New London, wherever he was stationed, to care for their children, first Jack, then Chip, then Jeff. During these periods she could not rely upon her husband for parenting as Jimmy, as a child, had been unable to rely upon Miss Lillian. But perhaps because with his own children Carter wanted to try to reverse the experience of his own childhood, sea duty had the effect of placing Rosalynn in situations where she had no alternative but to do the mothering. Carter's naval career also meant that their life together was, in his words, "one of constant separations interspersed with ecstatic reunions."[37] It may be that this was the only way intimacy could be handled, that prolonged periods of close personal involvement with his wife were perceived as intolerable, that the ecstatic reunions somehow proved that their love still flourished. In any case, it was the only pattern of intimacy he had ever known.

In his naval career, the presumed closeness of Jimmy and Rosalynn, a theme repeated over and over by America's journalists, proves to be more a part of the current group-fantasy than of the Carter's lived reality. But the pattern of long absences punctuated by ecstatic reunions was itself to change, abruptly. With the death of his father Earl, in 1953, Jimmy resigned his commission, leaving a promising naval career to return to Plains. His decision meant that he and Rosalynn would be together constantly. His return to Plains caused their now-celebrated first major argument.

While their marriage had contained several features of Carter's own family experience, Jimmy and Rosalynn had developed a somewhat different family system, one which had found its own equilibrium. The return to Plains could only have been stressful. Earl's death was the crisis which caused Jimmy to regress to an earlier stage of development, awakening fears of abandonment from his still surviving parent, Miss Lillian. Fears were so marked that Jimmy had to return to his childhood home; to be close to his mother was more important than the promising naval career Jimmy had now abandoned. Personally, Rosalynn was untouched by the emotional consequences of the death of Jimmy's father (though it doubtless evoked memories of her own father's leukemia). Consequently, she was not as compulsively drawn to her former home town as was her husband. She had made a suitable adjustment to naval life and has indicated how much she had enjoyed the excitement of new places. Her world had been expanded: it was now suddenly constricted. Plains also meant competition and conflict with Miss Lillian and her own mother. Rosalynn fought hard for her life—but Jimmy won. And he won in a number of ways.

The Carters had undergone a *rite de passage* on July 5, 1946, they were married but had not yet created a marriage. They had had little opportunity to engage in the painful joy of give and take over a prolonged period of time, being together only momentarily, in bits and pieces, during their reunions. The return to Plains meant that they would have to establish a new relationship. It was as if they were forming a family for the first time.

Family therapists know that when partners marry they expect their marriage to take the forms with which they are familiar, those of their parents. Each partner will try to force the other's behavior into a mold learned earlier. Jimmy's response to the new situation was to expect Rosalynn to accommodate to the familiar pattern of his own upbringing: he assumed that she would adopt the role of physically distancing mother. She did. Rosalynn became the business bookkeeper, working for eighteen hours a day, leaving behind her three young children. In Jimmy's words, "Jeffrey was still a baby. Chip was three years old. Jack was a first grader." Her work was justified by the fact that Earl's business was in "trouble" (although he had left a sizeable estate) and earned only $187 in profits during Jimmy's first year of operation. It seems as if Jimmy's victory over Rosalynn was a turning point in their relationship, for it established a pattern which enabled him to mold her later into his image of the fugitive-parent political wife.

By all accounts Rosalynn Smith Carter, throughout most of her life as child and woman, had been shy and retiring.[38] Upon her husband's entering politics, Jimmy's expectations—especially in 1970—and her willingness to perform as an active political wife were to cause her to triumph over a lifetime of withdrawal.

Her reactions to functioning as Jimmy Carter's delegate in the early years of his political career, including the 1970 Georgia gubernatorial race, are beautifully recreated by Gail Sheehy from her interview with Rosalynn.

The terror would begin in the back of her throat, the dryness, the feeling that the throat walls were closing in and her epiglottis was a stone. Along about halfway to the rally, she couldn't utter a word. Then the terror would burn its way down to her stomach and the nausea would begin. Sometimes, she had to stop the car and get out. Just the anticipation of standing up before an audience, for the first time in her life, to make a formal speech, *in Jimmy Carter's place,* made her physically ill . . . "It was," she said, "the hardest thing I'd ever had to do in my life."[39]

But she did it despite the terror and in the process left behind her year-and-a-half-old daughter, Amy. It is not the only reason, but Jimmy Carter's model of his mother as fugitive parent had to be adopted by Rosalynn Carter despite her own discomforts.

While campaigning for the presidency in the last two years, both have continued their lifetime pattern of family avoidance, returning to Plains only on weekends. Miss Lillian has been charged, as Jimmy charged Rosalynn in his Navy days, with "caring" for his child.

The national group-fantasy cannot admit that Amy Carter may have been unhappy with this situation. As Charlotte Curtis wrote in *McCall's*: "Amy happily stayed with her [grandmother] when her parents were away."[40] Yet, there are numerous indications that Amy missed both her parents deeply. In describing Amy for *Ms. Magazine,* Miss Lillian reported: "And she's very smart and very shrewd. And she knows the seriousness of Jimmy's race. She doesn't blame them for leaving her all the time. She cries a little bit every time, but the minute they leave, she'll say, 'Grandma, well, I'm glad to get back. I hate for my mama to leave, but I know she has to.'"[41] However, full confirmation of Amy Carter's real feelings comes to us from her interview with *Children's Express.*

In the eleven-year-old *Express* reporter's analysis of Amy, we seem to hear echos of earlier Carters. "Some people say that since she is shy and quiet and sort of reserved that she is dumb or something like that, but that's not true, she's very bright. She's just very quiet and sort of inward and self-contained, so that's why she didn't talk much." This assessment evokes memories of Jimmy as a boy and of Rosalynn's childhood and pre-political adult life. Did Amy miss her father, asked the *Express*? "Yes. He usually campaigns for a week and then comes home for the weekend." Perhaps Amy's most significant comment came in response to the question of whether her life had changed much since her father had begun his run at the presidency. "No," she said, "but I go with my mother sometimes to campaign. We went to Chicago, Maine and New Hampshire, and New York and Oregon." Amy's life had not changed, "but" she now "sometimes" went with her mother. Had it been that she had not accompanied her often in the past? Amy's words reveal the natural excitement of a child visiting new places. That she remembers *exactly* where she accompanied her mother may be the result of the fact that she was then very much with her. Of course Amy has repressed and denied. "Was it just the same when your father was governor?" asked the *Express.* "Well, I don't know 'cause I was only two years old when he ran for governor."[42] But (the psychohistorian must conclude), Amy does know. Somewhere within her are memories of earlier campaigns, of long hours of her parents at work at their respective desks in the governor's mansion, of absences which, to a child's mind, can sometimes seem interminable. Rosalynn must also have transmitted much of the anxiety she felt upon becoming the First Lady of Georgia: "I had this thing about wanting my hair and nails to be perfect . . . I felt as if people were looking at me. Amy was three and I drove myself nearly crazy trying to keep her perfect. I thought I had to be perfect, and I couldn't do it."[43]

As a husband and as a parent, Jimmy Carter has recapitulated the flight-from-home model of Miss Lillian which he had experienced in his childhood. Despite the relatively scanty evidence now available on what actually took place during his early boyhood, powerful confirmation of Miss Lillian's role as a distancing parent comes to us from her own adult behavior, from the brief glimpses we have of the biographical material of other members of the Carter family, and from Jimmy Carter's own style of parenting. What Miss Lillian's fear of intimacy, withdrawal and flight-from-home behavior did to her children's emotional development is an issue of tremendous complexity. We can only suggest here a few of the ways in which the new President responded to his mother's treatment.

SOME CONSEQUENCES FOR CARTER'S PERSONALITY

Current accounts from those who knew him best confirm Carter's early emotional controls. Not unnaturally, the *Children's Express* reporters were interested in whether he was a troublesome child. Was he well-behaved? Ninety-year-old Miss Rachel Clark, who helped raise him, said: "He didn't bother nobody. He was a quiet boy, a very good one." What was he like as a child? Alton Carter, Jimmy's eighty-eight-year-old uncle replied: "Just as nice as you ever saw." Was he involved in any mischief? Alton's son and Jimmy's cousin, Georgia State Senator Hugh

Carter remembered: "No, I can't think of any. He just read all the time." Was he ever in trouble? Answered Miss Lillian: "No . . . everybody asks what did he do bad, and he was a pretty good little country boy. Just a little red-headed freckle-faced boy who lived in the country."[44]

Jimmy has translated the extreme control pattern of his childhood into a positive virtue. It was a pattern which came to be imposed on his own children and has been carried over into his presidency. According to Gloria's son, Willie Carter Spann, Jimmy's nephew, when he lived briefly with the family, he was surprised to find that "There was even a little dressing area in the kids' bathroom . . . We were all boys living there—their daughter, Amy, hadn't been born yet—but we couldn't be seen naked in front of each other." Such absolute dominance of other's lives is reflected in Carter's current conduct of cabinet meetings, with the members of his cabinet perhaps cast in the role of children. Except for Health, Education and Welfare Secretary Joseph Califano, Jr., and Ambassador to the United Nations Andrew Young, who offer some resistance to Carter's ideas, the rest of the cabinet "just sit there," reported an unnamed source in the *New York Times,* "go through their little recitations of what's happening in their departments and nod agreeably when the President speaks."[45] Carter must not only strive for total self-control, he must also feel in control of those around him.

As a child, Jimmy was probably unable to express any feelings of anger toward either of his parents. Lillian gave Jimmy an occasional spanking but Earl loomed largest in Jimmy's mind as the formal family disciplinarian. According to *Why Not the Best?,* Earl was the man who "I never even considered disobeying," and who "punished me severely when I misbehaved." Between the ages of four and fifteen, Jimmy was, in his word, "whipped" by Earl at least six times (there may have been more) and recounts three of the six incidents in detail. He vividly remembers the instrument of punishment, "a small, long, flexible peach tree switch." Once he was "switched" for stealing a penny from a church collection-plate; another time, unable to sleep because loud voices emanating from his parents' party drove him to sleep in a treehouse outdoors, for refusing to answer his father's call to return inside. Whatever else the incidents reveal, Jimmy was punished for "disobeying" authority. He learned to be extremely responsive to parental wishes and to respond quickly without complaint: Earl "seldom if ever ordered me to perform a task; he simply suggested that it needed to be done, and he expected me to do it."[46]

In such an environment, expressions of childish anger had to be repressed. But the anger had to go someplace. Part of it was directed into hard work, a Carter characteristic which seems to be shared by everyone in the family and dovetails neatly into the American work ethic. Part of it, perhaps most of it, was directed inwardly against the self. This seems to account, in part, for the Carter family's tendency to take physical risks.

At age 68, as a member of the Peace Corps, Miss Lillian traveled to disease-ravaged India, returning two years later more than thirty pounds underweight. The president's oldest sister, Gloria Carter Spann, a motorcycle enthusiast, has become notorious for her eighty-mile-per-hour tears along the backroads of southwest Georgia. In a touching autobiographical vignette, she tells us how, after years of deep involvement with religious retreats, she resolved to spend more time with her family: "When I got home, I greeted my husband saying, 'Walter, if you'll get me a motorcycle, I'll learn to ride it.' (I don't know why I chose motorcycling, it just popped into my head.)" Rosalynn, at least once during the campaign, flew to a political rally in a private aircraft after its malfunctioning engine had been repaired by a local farmer.[47] And the President's younger brother, Billy, escaped Plains as an adolescent in the 1950's by joining the United States Marines, who had and have the reputation of being the toughest, the first in, and the ones who took the biggest casualties in combat.

As for Jimmy himself, risk-taking seems to account for his fascination with the only spectator sport he follows with regularity.

I've been a fan for the last 30 years. When I was in the Navy in New York, Rosy and I used to go to the dirt tracks in northern New York. Then back in Georgia we used to drive down to Sebring and stay in the back of our station wagon for a few days. We'd go to Daytona a lot too. We know all the race-car drivers. When I was governor, we had a banquet at the mansion every year for all the race drivers . . . I used to study different cars. I have records of automobile engines that I listen to. We know all the pit crews and engineers. Sometimes, we visit the pit crews during the races.[48]

Much could be said about the symbolic significance of automotive sport—beautiful women and champagne in the winner's circle, the hypnotic, repetitive circling in an enclosed oval, the total isolation of the race driver, the union of man and machine, the masculine and feminine sexual symbolism, the fantasies of great power, the dangers to drivers and spectators alike. It is enough to notice here that the racing driver—like the astronaut riding a volcano—is the master of a controlled, directed fury in which one missed step, one miscue means disaster. It is the test of skill, the challenge of raw nerve that the spectator vicariously enjoys—and perhaps the semi-expectation of the spill, the crack-up, the flames, oblivion. "I don't know why I like it," Carter has said. "I don't like to drive fast myself."[49]

Jimmy may not enjoy speeding frantically about the hills, but he has indulged in other kinds of risks in his life. Not only did he embrace a naval career, but he chose one of the most dangerous jobs in the service, submarines. Later, aware of the threats of nuclear power, he became part of the team which would build America's arsenal of nuclear subs. In his first venture into politics—which successfully challenged a fixed election—Carter was apparently not intimidated by not-so-veiled threats of bodily injury. On a camping trip-vacation while Governor, Carter was half of the first canoe tandem to ever successfully negotiate the Bull Sluice, a 150-foot run of rapids (including two almost six-foot vertical waterfalls) on the Chattooga River, a feat which prompted Atlanta journalist John Pennington to remark: "He's like a kid who steps on a potato vine to see if it's a snake." In the early days of the New Hampshire primary, Carter arrived early one morning at an airport in a raging snow storm only to find his pilot chipping ice from the wings of his private plane. His advisors tried to dissuade him from taking off. Shaking off their protests with the phrase, "People are waiting for me," he flew out into the blinding storm anyway. Stories of the Secret Service's frustrations in dealing with Carter were circulating before he became president, and on January 2 a radio news report indicated how irked the Service was by Carter's preference for flying into and out of Plains from a grass-strip airfield owned by a friend.[50] But the most striking example of Carter's willingness to take risks remains the most remarkable event of Inauguration Day. We still remember Vice President Mondale, seated in an armored, bullet-proof limousine, following the Carters as they walked for the mile-and-a-half from the Capitol to the White House. It was a fitting act for the "People's Inaugural" and merged nicely with Carter's image as a populist. It made Walter Cronkite feel "in awe of this performance." In light of recent American history, it may not have been the wisest course, but it fit perfectly into the risk-pattern of Carter's life.

Another way in which Carter has dealt with his feelings of maternal loss and maternal distancing has been to internalize maternal functions. Without a mother he has become his own mother and performs domestic duties himself. Pridefully, Rosalynn proclaimed that "Jimmy really likes to cook, and likes to help—he's pretty liberated." On his Plains weekends during the campaign, he consistently made the beds and fixed breakfast, usually of grits and eggs, sausage and bacon. The wife of prominent New Yorker, Howard Samuels, has entertained Carter as an overnight houseguest and reports that, "He is a pleasant, considerate guest—who makes his own bed." His domesticity was reconfirmed by Barbara Walters when, before a pre-inaugural interview with the Carters, she noted that they have a part-time maid, but do most of the cooking and cleaning themselves. During the campaign some observers were openly cynical of Carter's grooming habits and found it curious that he washed out his own shirts every evening. The *Playboy* interview recounts another example of domesticity, unusual in a presidential candidate. *"Playboy:* Say do you always do your own sewing? *(This portion of the interview took place aboard a plane. As he answered the interviewer's questions, Carter had been sewing a rip in his jacket with a needle and thread he carried with him.)* Carter: Uh-huh. *(He bit off the thread with his teeth.)"*[51]

Carter's current domesticity can be admired as "liberation" and rationalized as part of his self-reliance. Yet in the light of the other evidence it appears likely that, like others who perceive themselves as rejected children, he has compensated for a sensed maternal object loss by incorporating into himself some of the behavior defined as maternal by American society. By preparing his own foods and washing and repairing his own clothing, Jimmy has reduced the anxiety provoked by childhood memories of uncertain maternal care. His physical needs will be surely met if he takes care of them himself.

Because Carter has tried to internalize a nurturant image he has been able to use it, perhaps unconsciously, throughout his political career. It is a face that has served him well. Even as Georgia governor he projected a fantasied maternal image of nurturance and caring. Gary Wills recalled in a pre-election reminiscence how Carter had acted four years before while addressing a convention of Georgia sheriffs in 1972. His words were "almost crooned into the microphone," said Wills, and brought to the Georgia sheriffs a message "of love for God and one's fellow man." The message seemed "A persuasive lullaby" that worked remarkably well "on a tough yet vulnerable audience of mean shits and neighbors." In the process Carter was "using the voice of each sheriff's schoolmarm or mother, telling him how important it is to wash behind his ears." In a post-election evaluation, Wills returned to the same theme he had used over six months before, calling Carter's election-even speech at Illinois' Quad City Airport a "magnified coo of love."[52] It is what America wanted to hear.

PSYCHOHISTORICAL FACTORS
IN CARTER'S PRESIDENTIAL VICTORY

At this stage in our group process Americans do not want a stern, demanding father figure (although Carter seems able to fill that role), as much as they long for a loving, caring, nurturant leader.

The wishes of this peculiarly utopian group-fantasy were momentarily verbalized by Carter in the first line of his Inaugural speech, a line which drew the most thunderous and sustained applause of any in the address: "For myself and for our nation, I want to thank my predecessor for all he has done to heal our land." In 1976 the group-fantasy could not tolerate a presidential campaign in which one or both candidates were witty, sophisticated and urbane. America wanted presidential candidates who were honest, caring family men, able to create the illusion of caring and nurturance without stimulating the anxiety which would be provoked by vigorously attacking the many serious problems confronting America and by initiating far-reaching fundamental reforms in American society. It turned out that Jimmy Carter was better able to convince us that he was more "down-home folks" than Gerald Ford. It is an image, and a need, which endure.

In almost every *New York Daily News* headline reporting on the President, the already familiar "Jimmy" has been abbreviated to the even more familiar "Jim." Most observers have commented on Carter's restoration of the Fireside Chat as a device designed to link him in our minds to a favored presidential predecessor, Franklin Delano Roosevelt. This may account for it—consciously. That it also fulfills the wishes of the group-fantasy is suggested by the headline: "Carter Will Cozy Up to Us With a Fireside TV Chat."[53] The President's adoption of casual clothing reinforced the aura of informality as we were invited into his home. Later he came to us by attending a New England Town Meeting. And underlying the rational statements of the March 5 two-hour presidential call-in "Ask President Carter," when he came to us again, was a group-fantasy message of nurturance and caring. Some of the functional words in Carter's replies were: "protected . . . assurance . . . not be hurt . . . reinforce . . . personally care about . . . concerned . . . security . . . not suffer . . . supported strengthening . . . interest . . . concern . . . insure . . . encourage . . . support," many, especially "concern" and "support" repeated over and over again.[54]

Through these efforts, Carter seems to be caring for us, seems interested in our problems and seems to be making us part of his family. The President is thus fulfilling the tasks delegated to him by the group-fantasy, a task summarized in a pre-Inaugural interview with the President-elect and Rosalynn by Barbara Walters. Near the end of her interview, Walters quietly asked Carter to "be wise with us . . . be good to us."[55] Morley Safer and other journalists were outraged by what they considered Walters' unprofessional editorializing, but her plea perfectly reflected the desires of the current group-fantasy.

But Carter's image as a nurturant leader, carried out by him and projected onto him by the present American group-fantasy, is not the only psychohistorical reason for his November, 1976 presidential victory.

To many, Carter's public personality, developed by his advisors over the last four years, is an almost ideal type. Jimmy is rich and successful. He ran for the presidency and was successful. His successes came because he was hard-working, self-controlled and intensely competitive. He has come from obscurity to prominence by his own efforts: he has told us so.

He is a man of high moral principles and high idealism. In his public image he loves his family and finds refuge in it. As a farmer, he is close to nature and to the soil and appreciates the simple virtues. He upholds motherhood. His individualism is tempered by a constantly reiterated concern for his fellow human beings.

Recognizable in all of this is a personality, or psychological type, that was glorified in nineteenth-century America, an ideal that the parents of Jimmy Carter admired and emulated and succeeded in instilling in him. Even in the nineteenth century, this ideal type was something of a myth, yet it is precisely the mythic illusion that America has responded to as the group-fantasy has endowed Carter with fantasied qualities from our idealized nineteenth-century past.

Psychohistorians have begun to recognize that group life proceeds through a series of distinct stages. One of those stages has been identified as a phase in which the group feels lost, purposeless and leaderless, sometimes stemming from a sense of leadership betrayal. This evokes rage in group members and awakens primitive fears of fragmentation and extinction. One response to these fears in the utopian fantasy of return to an idealized past of group cohesion and purposefulness to be engineered by a purified outsider—the "messiah."

In the last fifteen years America has "lost" at least two Presidents, John F. Kennedy and Richard Nixon. One defensive response to the shock of Kennedy's death was the emergence of the Camelot myth. The shared psychohistorical experience of the Watergate trauma, itself a painful moment, reawakened memories of Kennedy's earlier "abandonment." The Ford pardon did little to alleviate the psychological shock of Nixon's betrayal and loss. It is something Carter and his staff had vaguely recognized and during the campaign Carter became partly responsible for feeding America's messiah-expectation. Echoing an important emotional state in his own early years ("During my childhood I never considered myself a part of Plains society, but always thought of myself as a visitor when I entered that 'metropolitan' community"),[56] Carter in the First Debate reiterated a major theme of the campaign, one he had repeatedly emphasized, that he was not part of the Washington establishment but would be "coming in as an outsider," a characteristic of the "messiah." Carter openly admitted in the campaign that his "frankness might very well not be a good safe thing to do in a political campaign,"[57] but still built his image as a kind of poor man's charismatic leader through continued openness and honesty, presuming they would win for him in November. Reflecting this element of the group-fantasy was the title of a campaign biography, *The Miracle of Jimmy Carter.* In May, 1976, the *New Republic* wondered: "Is there a connection between his promise never to lie to you, never to deceive you, and the response he is getting after Watergate?"[58] Psychohistory answers this question not with impressions, but with theories derived from empirical evidence from small group research. The answer is yes: after groups lose their leader, they often fear disintegration, and look for an outsider to serve as a utopian-fantasy leader.

Thus, despite the fact that some Americans are put off by Carter's frankness, his religious earnestness, or whatever other doubts inform our prejudices, Carter symbolizes a fantasied return to our pre-industrial, pre-urban, pre-modern, problem-free past, a fantasy of rural honesty, moral purpose and "just-Plains-folks" clanishness. It is rural America of the nineteenth century returned.

Part of Carter's magic lies in our perception of him as a kind of frontiersman-hero. The *New York Daily News* even referred to him as "the Plainsman." His dedication to guns, his quail hunting, his denim dress, his affection for square dancing, his farming (a nurturant symbol) and the Huckleberry Finn-like boyhood portrayed in *Why Not the Best?* all carry us into the frontier fantasy. It has not only been Jimmy Carter who has been consciously identified as the bearer of the frontier mythology. It has also been attached to Rosalynn, who has been imbued with a frontier mystique. "Rosalynn Smith Carter reminds me of those pioneer women who left the comforts of hearth and home to join the rugged trip to the unknown West," wrote Charlotte Curtis. "A breed of women who hadn't the vaguest idea of the hardship ahead, but who faced up to their inexperience, their terrors and all that a capricious wilderness could throw at them, survived and, the stronger for the ordeal, moved a civilization forward." We might diagnose such judgments as the romantic idealization expected from women's magazines like *McCalls*. What, then, is one to make of Gail Sheehy in the sophisticated *New York Magazine*? "Sister Rosalynn is the very essence of the pioneer wife, the kind you've seen in the 'big sky' movies, the one who draws a weary hand across her brow at the end, straightens her apron, picks up the drowned child, and walks back through the drought-stricken fields to the cabin, determined to get the seed in the ground for next season."[59] In addition to Rosalynn as pioneer-wife, we notice Sheehy's imagery of the drowned child and drought-stricken fields and recognize that, on unconscious levels, they might easily symbolize modern America in the current group-fantasy.

The Carters as fulfillment and recreation of our frontier myth blends neatly into another of America's historical fictions out of the nineteenth century—the rags-to-riches Horatio Alger story. Few, if any, of today's hard-headed, cynical Americans actually believe, consciously, that just anyone can become President of the United States. We would like to believe that we have left that myth forever behind us. But in the process we lament the passing, as does *Roots* author Alex Haley in the official 1977 Presidential Inaugural book. "In recent years it has sometimes seemed to the American People as if power goes mainly to the powerful, wealth to those that have no need of it, education to the sons and daughters of the educated. And the old hope that any child might grow up to be President has come to seem a little foolish." Yet today, Haley implies, all is not lost. "Not since the nineteenth century has a Southerner and farmer come to the White House."[60] The popularity of the film *Rocky* reveals the rags-to-riches theory is still a money making format, and in one of the first post-election books promising to reveal the reasons for Carter's success, Davis Newton Lott's paperback picture-book *Jimmy Carter and How He Won,*[61] the Carter "miracle" is reflected in a headline running from the inside front cover to page 1: "FROM PLAINS TO PENNSYLVANIA AVENUE," underneath, "AN IN-CREDIBLE STORY." "With the World As A Backdrop and Stage for this drama you will see woven before your eyes the fragile fabric of folklore your grandchildren will someday read and marvel: 'The Saga of Jimmy Carter' (and how he won our nation's highest honor against almost impossible odds.)" Even professional politicians have countered Carter's electoral success nothing short of miraculous.[62]

This brief elaboration of some of the reasons for Carter's victory—his nurturant image, his portrayal of self as an outsider, his ties to the frontier and Horatio Alger myths—has been trying to catch hold of vague, though powerful, unconscious themes in the group-fantasy. Psychohistory does not deny the importance of more traditional kinds of analyses from political science, but hopes to provide yet another dimension of understanding by interpreting psychological factors. Indeed, much energy has already been expended by political scientists in trying to assess precisely how and why Carter won in November. It is an important issue which will continue to preoccupy political scientists, historians and members of the Democratic and Republican National Committees. To psychohistorians, however, as important as the question of why Carter won at all is the question of why Carter won by so little.

THE NARROWNESS OF PRESIDENTIAL VICTORY

A close presidential election (2 percent of the popular vote in 1976) is a phenomenon hardly unknown in recent American history—we are reminded of the even narrower margin between Kennedy and Nixon in 1960—but in the past two hundred years, narrow presidential victories have been unusual in the United States. In the case of Carter-Ford there are many ways to account for the closeness of the popular vote, but lengthy statistical computer printouts and minute examinations of segmented voter behavior are not the only ways to find meaningful explanations. We must again turn to the realm of group process and to an analysis of modern America's group-fantasy.

The main reason for Carter's narrow margin of victory was not so much that he was a relative unknown (although that is part of it), as much as it was that the American electorate was unable to meaningfully differentiate between the two presidential candidates. The difficulty in differentiation goes beyond the familiar observation that there is little ideological difference between Republicans and Democrats in American politics: there are at least three other reasons for it.

Surely the Carter-Ford contest was conspicuous as a campaign without issues. The closest the candidates came to issue definition was on things like abortion and amnesty, but briefly, and Carter's "lust-in-the-heart" slip and Ford's "no-Soviet-domination-in-eastern-Europe" mistake were more media-inspired "non-issue" issues than anything else. That a number of observers noted a lack of seriousness in the campaign led to a flurry of charges and counter-charges in late October and early November. Earlier Carter had said that: "The national news media have absolutely no interest in issues at all. . . . There's nobody on the press plane who would ask an issue question unless he thought he could trick me into some crazy statement."[63] Ford too was critical of the press. In short, both blamed the media and the media blamed Ford and Carter, while David Susskind presented a post-election TV program on the subject of "Carter vs. Ford: the Media."

The scholarly approach is not to make charges and apportion blame but to recognize, from the standpoint of group-fantasy, that in historical process, as in personal interrelationships, people often get what they most want and that rational styles are first of all defensive. The efforts of Carter's and Ford's campaign strategists to tap the desires of the American people, and the media's obligation to report those stories that will sell their products, both suggest that the media and the candidates gave Americans what they most wanted—an issue-free campaign. When our deepest fears are reflected by cinematic fantasies of cosmic destruction, it seems clear that in the mid-'70s, perhaps more than in the previous decade, we are not ready to welcome realistic reminders of serious issues. The electorate's denial of painful problems is surely as responsible as the media and the candidates for the issueless campaign of 1976.

A second reason for our difficulty in distinguishing between the candidates (hence Carter's narrow margin of victory) lies in the tendency of American politicians to campaign with images, not issues. Both Ford and Carter failed to satisfactorily project their prepackaged selves. Ford's was the "father image," the "good," "kind" man, the experienced "insider" possessed of a balanced, if mundane, style who would never rock the boat by risking change. Carter's was the "savior image," the man who "couldn't lie," the "outsider" who owed no one anything and who could then engender hope and confidence in America by restoring morality, but somehow doing so without being overly activist.

These "media myths," designed by the media experts, were doubtless sharply enough defined—in the minds of the media experts. The problem was that they just didn't work for America. Ford and Carter are politicians, not professional actors, and are not going to win any Oscars. Uncomfortable in their prearranged roles, and not quite convinced themselves of their prefigured images, they could not be wholly convincing to the public.

Without sharply-drawn issues and without effectively projected images, the question of the presidential election of 1976 was ultimately reduced to the personalities of the two candidates. Indeed, it had been Carter's "personality" which had won the Democratic nomination in the first place. As political scientist Walter Dean Burnham noted in mid-July, "Carter's capture of the Democratic party was the most strikingly personal victory in our modern electoral history."[64] Carter's persistent hard work, and the fact that he came from nowhere, recall his first political success in getting elected to the Georgia State Legislature and his later victory as Georgia governor. We already know psychohistorically that politicians tend to relive the kind of campaigns that brought them their first political victory. We might have expected that the 1976 elections would be resolved by personality.

What was in the characters of both candidates that led to confusion about their respective merits in the minds of the American people? What was it that caused Carter's margin of victory to be so narrow?

While we enter here into extremely speculative terrain, it may well have been that on a deep level of consciousness Americans understood that the essential feature of both presidential candidates in 1976 was a personal history both may have shared in common. Their adult personalities may have been forged out of somewhat similar traumata.

There is no psychohistorical study of Gerald Ford, and even extant biographies leave much untouched,[65] yet Ford's childhood experience, at least on the surface, was marked by a dramatic incident which may have significantly influenced his adult behavior. Sometime after he was born Leslie King, Jr., in 1913, Ford's natural father left the family and dropped out of sight only to resurface with peculiar suddenness when Ford was seventeen years old. When Ford was two, his mother obtained a divorce and subsequently remarried Gerald Ford, Sr., changing her son's name. There is no empirical evidence so far for the kind of parenting style employed by Ford's mother, but the early experience of abandonment, and perhaps later unconscious reminders of it throughout his childhood (Ford denies conscious knowledge of the event), may have molded him on some level into the same kind of personality as Jimmy Carter.

If so, it may have been this that the American electorate identified with in 1976. Because the Ford and Carter family histories resonated with Watergate—America's own trauma of abandonment—both candidates were almost equally acceptable to the American public. Their personal traumas—but Jimmy's more so—corresponded to our national trauma. As psychohistorian Rudolf Binion has demonstrated in another connection, it is the coincidence of personal history with public trauma which accounts for much of the dynamic interaction in history betweem political leaders and their followers, otherwise the potential leader would come away from his trauma, writes Binion, "about like the next traumatic casualty before or after him: hellbent on reliving his traumatic experience, but without that imperative engaging anyone else."[66] It was Watergate which "engaged" us in the traumatic reliving of "abandoned" son Gerald Ford and distanced son Jimmy Carter, chosen by us in 1976 to represent our own abandoned selves.

In this traumatic engagement Jimmy Carter had a conspicuous advantage. It appears that he was better able than Gerald Ford to cope with his trauma, having internalized maternal functions early in life and having unconsciously utilized the nurturant part of himself in politics even as Georgia governor. Ford's "Nice-Guy Jerry" image, was, like Carter's healing image, a response to the aftermath of Watergate and post-Watergate revelations of leadership betrayal. While projecting nurturance, Ford was too much the kindly father-figure; what America yearned for was maternal-like nurturance. The shared traumas of America's psychohistorical experience were too deep and had forced the group to regress to much earlier levels of experience where only an image of compassionate maternal nurturance could accommodate the group-fantasy.

In his two years as President, Gerald Ford may have relived his own personal trauma by acting out the same kind of abandonment that had occurred to him. He had "pardoned" Richard Nixon as he had "forgiven" his own father, but, like his natural father, he continued to "abandon" America by exercising the executive veto forty-two times. More than any other action, Ford's treatment of financially troubled New York City may have been interpreted as a microcosm and symbol of his relationship to America.

Ford denied that he had ever told New York City to "drop dead," yet his treatment of the city's fiscal difficulties with disdain amounted to the same thing. While many throughout the nation welcomed New York's financial problems as a deserving judgment for fiscal "mismanagement," many others did not. To the extent that individuals identified with New York City, Ford's behavior may well have had the impact of clouding America's already uncertain future: if he could abandon the country's artistic and financial capital, how about Little Rock? For some voters, New York's abandonment and Ford's vetos may have been enough to tip the scales away from paternalistic, "Nice-Guy-Jerry" to the more maternal, but uncertain, "savior" Jimmy.

For New York City, the group-fantasy of Carter as savior began to build toward Christmas, 1976. Just prior to the New Year, with its promise of renewal and revival, New York State's Governor Carey, New York City's Mayor Beame and the head of New York's Municipal Assistance Corporation, Felix Rohatyn, went, like pilgrims, to Carter's St. Simon's Island retreat. Upon their return to Manhattan, the three officials were filled with enthusiasm, Governor Carey claiming that Carter had "assured us that the partnership of the federal government will be there under his administration," Mayor Beame stating that, "He's going to help, the partnership is there." Both believed the President-elect was "not going to let the city down." Less restrained, but more suggestive of the feelings of the city and the country was Felix Rohatyn, who enthused: "we have a patron who won't let us fall off the cliff." In addition to the anxiety-birth imagery of falling off a cliff (which suggests how far his own fears had forced him to regress), Rohatyn employed language indicative of the abandoned child, language which reveals expectations of reestablished family harmony. "We've basically been readopted back into the United States and it's very refreshing," he said. Summarizing the group-fantasy, and evoking the earlier Ford-inspired headline, was the *New York Daily News'* lead covering the story: "Carter to City: You'll Never Drop Dead." The reality was more accurately revealed two months later in *New York Magazine*'s cover story, "Carter to City: 'Heal Thyself'."[67] At the earlier moment, at the end of Christmas Week 1976 on the eve of the New Year, America's group-fantasy had to believe otherwise.

Like an omnipotent mother, Jimmy Carter represents to us a defense against myriad dangers. It may not have been altogether coincidental that the very day following Carter's inauguration saw the New York revival of *Jaws,* one of the most popular films of our time. As part of popular culture, films, and their connection to the ongoing group process, have already begun to be investigated by psychohistorians.[68] Whatever else the film might mean, in *Jaws* we have fashioned out of our inner selves a devouring sea-beast symbolizing in a nuclear age the possibility of sudden destruction in the most secure lagoon. The group-fantasy sees the President as an alternative to the monster. One cartoon depicts "Evel Kjimmy" soaring on a motorcycle over snapping shark's teeth.[69] In a daredevil ride Carter magically carries himself, and us, to safety despite a multitude of potentially fatal encounters.

The present group-fantasy and Carter's desire to aid us are perfectly matched. In him, the conscious desire to help others, an unconscious identification with his mother's nursing career, had been repressed for many years and seems to have surfaced after his 1966 "conversion" experience, brought on, in part, by his mother's flight to India. The "conversion" experience was sparked by a need to prove to himself that he was not depressed, that he was not worthless, that by merging with

Christ he could become a powerful helping-nurse. His need to appear nurturant then manifested itself as a private citizen in his evangelical missions to the north, first in Pennsylvania, then in Massachusetts,[70] and was eventually transferred into politics where, first as governor, then as President, Carter was able to appear to help even larger numbers of anonymous strangers.

In recent months Carter's nurturant-image has been transferred to the world. In its first weeks, the Carter Administration spoke out against repression in the Soviet Union, and the day after his triumphant appearance at a Town Meeting in Massachusetts (one of the two states in his earlier evangelical efforts), Carter spoke movingly of human rights at the United Nations even at the expense of putting a large obstacle in the way of the SALT talks. Paradoxically, if Carter achieves his conception of America as his new family (as we want him to) the President may be driven from his task as apparent domestic healer onto the broader world stage where he may wish to perform the same kind of functions his mother had performed outside her family in the community of Plains. Miss Lillian's flight to India and Ruth Carter Stapleton's world-wide evangelical mission already serve as models, both achieved at the expense of their families, and wherever global troubles appear the President seems to want to exercise his nurturant image. These efforts have already received criticism from some segments of American society since some perceive his foreign policy approach (as Jimmy understood Miss Lillian's extra-familial commitments) as a kind of refusal to take care of business at home. In the long run Carter may be caught in a bind: the more successfully he fulfills our fantasy-expectations by creating a feeling of family involvement in America, the more likely may be his tendency to expend greater energies in trying to affect the world situation.

On one level we do not want Jimmy to leave us. It is the anxiety which lay behind the fact that television viewers saw more of his Inaugural than any other in history. It made good political sense, in the words of one Carter staffer, to gear "this Inaugural entirely toward the media," and it fit Carter's image as a populist if, through electronic gadgetry, we could be made somehow to believe the illusion that we participated in it. But there was more. In its Inaugural preview, *TV Guide* reported that for the first time a "camera will be allowed 'about 25 feet in front of President Carter as he sits in the reviewing stand,' according to an Inaugural spokesman, 'so that the people will be able to see—from his side of the street—how he's reacting to what's going on around him.' "[71] An anxious America seemed ready to hang on every smile, every frown, every gesture. Like the totalizing child who clings desperately to the formerly separated parent, America seems to have feared the danger that a President might be leaving us again.

As we have seen, the immediate causes for these feelings were Watergate and Nixon's resignation, but much else lies behind them. Whatever the ultimate group-fantasy reasons for Vietnam and Watergate prove to be (they have yet to be detailed), Nixon's landslide victory in 1972 created the illusion of unity, while the opening of relations with China and the close of the Vietnam War created the illusion of peace. As Nixon was caught in a shoddy drama of deceit and betrayal, America's sense of outrage was intensified, and in disgrace, the Big Daddy of the Imperial Presidency was forced to leave. America has dealt with these traumas by totalizing experience ("everything is rotten") while the conventional wisdom that "all politicians are corrupt" has resurfaced with a vengeance. While already a pattern of the '60s, partly as a way of refuting and eluding these traumatic shocks, and in order to gain some measure of "control" over their lives, Americans have increasingly embraced new mysticisms, Karmic beliefs, fatalistic philosophies and astrology. Many have become, in the "blame word" of the '70s, totally "apathetic." Underlying these responses is a sense of impotence accompanied by deep feelings of aloneness and abandonment.

No better measure of the mood of America on the eve of the presidential election exists than the emotional meaning of a major show mounted by New York City's Metropolitan Museum of Art in the fall of 1976. The show, a retrospective exhibit of the paintings of Andrew Wyeth, ran concurrently with the presidential campaign and drew thousands of people in a matter of months. Aesthetic judgements aside, Wyeth's work, filled with empty rooms, half-open doors, and brooding rural landscapes, evokes a haunting loneliness. By choosing him, the Metropolitan Museum perfectly reflected America's emptiness, a loneliness and emptiness eerily recreated, in the Wyeth tradition, by Georgia artist Butler Brown, the favorite painter of Rosalynn and Jimmy Carter. With it, America's mood and Carter's interior life are joined in yet another way and, in an even more striking connection, the Wyeth-Brown-Carter conjunction is heightened by what appears to be the only painting Jimmy Carter ever did—a personless, barren landscape.[72]

A final indicator of Carter's meaning to America, and an insight into part of the psychohistorical reason for his victory, may be seen in the personal reaction of novelist Reynolds Price to an evening with the Carters before the Inauguration. Price, reflecting on his emotional state, concluded his piece for *Time*'s "Man of the Year" issue with words that condense the essence of America's group fantasy. "With all the cold fears our past four Presidents have drenched us in, all the seedy disbeliefs they've sowed, I left . . . that night feeling better for my own kin's chances now and lighter on my feet, which slid in Georgia mud—purple Sumter County clay, the ground of many Carters over 125 years; apparently a national family at last to feed us with stories and the actions they cause: varied fare and nutritious, the stories of care and honest consolation that we've needed for very much longer than was good."[73]

Roots, continuity, a suggestion of royalty ("purple Sumter County clay"), at least—and at last—a national family. The Carters, peanut farmers and feed merchants, will feed us with nutritious and varied fare, give us care and honest consolation for our pain and what we have lost. As a people, Americans have been abandoned and alone for very much longer than was good. The burden was lifted as Price left light on his feet feeling better for his own kins' chances. In this way the presidency of an emotionally distanced Georgia boy and the despair of an abandoned and betrayed America are finally conjoined.

Emotional distance and parental loss run like a thread throughout the Carter family history. Each Carter generation has recapitulated the same recurrent trauma: by reliving it they have sought to master it. Now individual ego (Carter's presidency) and collective process (our feelings of governmental betrayal) are united in ways in which Gerald Ford, who could have approximated it, could not have achieved.

But can Jimmy Carter really care for us, nurture us, not leave us? Will his own personality force him to once again repeat the pattern of abandonment that he and his family seem to have been repeating for at least two generations? It has been Carter's childhood experience which molded him into a kind of "perfect" democratic President, a perfect reflector of America's group process. It is the image of nurturance, not the substance of reform, which the group-fantasy calls for: apparently we cannot now tolerate the anxiety-provoking activity that made the '60s a decade of turmoil. Yet the suspicion persists that the group traumas of assassination and Vietnam, Kent State, Jackson State and Watergate, which we somehow helped create, will not be resolved with cooing words of love and fantasies of nurturance. Unless we deal realistically with public traumas in our private selves, the group-fantasy may shift again and America may recapitulate a theatre of the absurd scenario in which future generations continue to relive, in distorted and altered form, the traumas of Vietnam, Kent State and Watergate again, and again and again.

David R. Beisel, Ph.D., Associate Professor in the Department of Social Science/Psychology at Rockland Community College, State University of New York, is a Research Associate of the Institute for Psychohistory, a Contributing Editor to The Journal of Psychohistory *and Convention Chairman of the International Psychohistorical Association. He is presently at work on a book-length psychohistorical study of President Jimmy Carter.*

REFERENCES

1. Carter's campaign autobiography *Why Not the Best?* (Nashville, Tenn.: Broadman Press, 1975) remains the major source for his early childhood and later memories, but, like all memoirs, especially those written for a political purpose, should be used with great caution. References here are to the widely distributed paperback edition (Toronto, New York and London: Bantam Books, 1976). For the concept and application of the idea of historical group-fantasy, see Lloyd deMause, "The Independence of Psychohistory" *History of Childhood Quarterly: The Journal of Psychohistory* 3 (Fall, 1975), 163-183, and his "The Formation of the American Personality Through Psychospeciation," *The Journal of Psychohistory* 4 (Summer, 1976), 1-30. For applications of group process to theory see Robert Denton Rossel, "Micro-History: Studying Social Change in the Laboratory," *History of Childhood Quarterly: The Journal of Psychohistory* 3 (Winter, 1976) 373-400, and the long review essay by John J. Hartmann, "Disasters, Utopias and Small Groups," *History of Childhood Quarterly: The Journal of Psychohistory* 3 (Spring, 1976), 552-564. Except for a few brief excursions into pop-psychology, the major books so far published on Carter have not adopted any psychohistorical perspectives: they are sometimes helpful for bits of empirical evidence but are mostly reflective of various elements of group-fantasy. As of this writing (May, 1977) the best book on Carter's campaign (and the best book on Carter) is Martin Schram, *Running for President 1976: The Carter Campaign* (New York: Stein and Day, 1977), Book I of which originally appeared as *Running for President: A Journal of the Carter Campaign* (New York: Pocket Books, 1976). Also helpful as straight political biography is Leslie Wheeler, *Jimmy Who?* (Woodbury, New York: Barron's, 1976), and, for insights into members of the Carter family, Kandy Stroud, *How Jimmy Won: The Victory Campaign From Plains to the White House* (New York: William Morrow, 1977). Campaign biographies includes the anti-Carter Jeffrey St. John, *Jimmy Carter's Betrayal of the South* (Ottowa, Illinois: Green Hill Publishers, 1976), the sympathetic Tom Collins, *The Search for Jimmy Carter* (Waco, Texas: Word Books, 1976) and the religiously oriented Howard Norton and Bob Slosser, *The Miracle of Jimmy Carter* (Plainsfield, New Jersey: Logos International, 1976), and David Kucharsky, *The Man From Plains: The Mind and Spirit of Jimmy Carter* (New York: Harper and Row, 1976). For his religious orientation see Niels C. Nielson, Jr., *The Religion of President Carter* (New York & Nashville: Thomas Nelson, 1977).
2. *New York Daily News,* January 21, 1977, 3. The *News* contains the

kind of journalism that has been avoided by historians in favor of "newspapers of record," like *The New York Times* and the *Washington Post,* but is an excellent source for the group-fantasy (as are the *Times* and *Post*). It also sometimes carries important direct quotes which never appear in the newspapers of record.

3. Harriet van Horne, "The Carter Macho," *The New York Post,* February 14, 1977, 28.

4. (Toronto, New York and London, 1977).

5. Charlotte Curtis, "What Kind of First Lady Will She Be?" *McCall's Magazine* (January, 1977), 26; Johnny Carson, *The Tonight Show,* NBC-TV, January 11, 1977; *Time Magazine,* "It's A New Washington: The Carter's Move In," (February 7, 1977), cover; Interview with Democratic Delegate From Abroad Jack Loiello and wife Elaine, January 5, 1977.

6. Edward Shorter, the *Making of the Modern Family* (New York: Basic Books, 1975).

7. Salvador Minuchin, *Families and Family Therapy* (Cambridge, Massachusetts: Harvard University Press, 1974), pp. 50-51.

8. James David Barber, "An Active-Positive Character," *Time Magazine* (January 3, 1977), 17. The Second Edition of Barber's, the *Presidential Character: Predicting Performance in the White House* (Englewood Cliffs, New Jersey: Prentice-Hall, 1977), contains a last chapter on President Carter but was published too late to be included in this paper.

9. Bruce Mazlish and Edwin Diamond, "Thrice-Born: A Psychohistory of Jimmy Carter's 'Rebirth'," *New York Magazine* (August 30, 1976), 26.

10. Ibid., 30.

11. "Billy Carter," *Who's Who,* CBS-TV, January 11, 1977.

12. *Why Not the Best?,* p. 13.

13. Peter Goldman, "Sizing up Carter," *Newsweek Magazine* (September 13, 1976), 26.

14. Patricia McCann interview with Ruth Carter Stapleton, *The Patricia McCann Show,* WOR Radio, January 13, 1977.

15. *The Children's Express* (February, 1977), 8; conversation with Paul Elovitz at the Stockton State College conference "Psychohistory: Present State, Future Prospect," October 15, 1976. The youthful journalists of *Children's Express* magazine obtained some important, if brief, interviews in Plains, Georgia, during the presidential campaign. The Carter family's genuine warmth toward children and the fact that they would likely be less guarded with children than with adults makes the *Express* interviews a key psychohistorical source.

16. Ruth Carter Stapleton, *The Gift of Inner Healing* (Waco, Texas:

Word, Incorporated, 1976), p. 17. A paperback edition has recently appeared (Toronto, New York & London: Bantam Books, 1977), with different pagination.

17. Glenn Davis, *Childhood and History in America* (New York: The Psychohistory Press, 1976).

18. Mazlish and Diamond, "Thrice-Born," 30; David Abrahamsen, *Nixon vs. Nixon: An Emotional Tragedy* (New York: Farrar, Straus and Giroux, 1977), Eli S. Chesen, *President Nixon's Psychiatric Profile* (New York: Peter H. Wyden, 1973), Bruce Mazlish, *In Search of Nixon: A Psychohistorical Inquiry* (Baltimore, Maryland: Penguin Books, 1973), James W. Hamilton, "Some Reflections on Richard Nixon in the Light of his Resignation and Farewell Speeches," *"The Journal of Psychohistory,"* 4 (Spring, 1977), 491)511.

19. *Why Not the Best?,* p. 12.

20. *Why Not the Best?,* p. 13; *Chidlren's Express,* 8; Goldman, "Sizing Up Carter," 26; *Why Not the Best?,* pp. 29-30. On the silver and gold stars for reading, Carter's May 4, 1974 Georgia Law Day speech excerpted in Robert W. Turner, ed., *"I'll Never Lie to You": Jimmy Carter in His Own Words* (New York: Ballantine Books, 1976), p. 19.

21. *New York Daily News,* January 21, 1977, 3.

22. "Billy Carter," *Who's Who.*

23. Ibid.; Bill Schemmel, "My Son Jimmy," *Ladies' Home Journal* (August, 1976), 73, 142; Mike Douglas interview with Lillian Carter *The Mike Douglas Show,* CBS-TV, December 13, 1976.

24. Reynolds Price, "Family Stories: The Carters in Plains," *Time Magazine* (January 3, 1977), 26; *Children's Express,* 10, 9.

25. Mike Douglas interview with Lillian Carter; William Greider, "The Carter Years," reprinted from *The Washington Post* in *The Rockland County Journal-News,* November 22, 1976, 6a; presentation of materials from an interview with Lillian Carter by Paul Elovitz at the Institute for Psychohistory's bi-monthly meeting, November 20, 1976.

26. Schemmel, "My Son Jimmy," 142.

27. "Lillian Carter Talks About Racism, The Kennedys, and Jimmy's Reign," *Ms. Magazine* (October, 1976), 88.

28. *Why Not the Best?,* p. 81.

29. deMause, "Formation of the American Personality,"; Joel Allison, "Religious Conversion: Regression and Progression in An Adolescent Experience," *Journal for the Scientific Study of Religion* 8 (Spring, 1969), 23-38.

30. Price, "Family Stories," 26, 29.

31. Minuchin, pp. 54-55.

32. Stapleton, p. 18.

33. McCann interview with Ruth Carter Stapleton.

34. Ibid.
35. Gloria Spann, "The Heartache of a Son Gone Wrong," *Good House-keeping* (January, 1977), 60, 63.
36. McCann interview with Ruth Carter Stapleton.
37. *Why Not the Best?,* p. 69.
38. Gail Sheehy, "Ladies and Gentlemen, The Second President—Sister Rosalynn," *New York Magazine* (November 22, 1976), 55.
39. Ibid., 56.
40. Curtis, "What Kind of First Lady," 26.
41. "Lillian Carter Talks," 92.
42. *Children's Express,* 7.
43. Curtis, "What Kind of First Lady," 26.
44. *Children's Express,* 8-10.
45. Willie Carter Spann with Burton H. Wolfe, "The Other Carter: Willie's Story in His Own Words (With a Little Help in Arrangement from Burton H. Wolfe)," *Hustler Magazine* (May, 1977), 52; James T. Wooten, "Carter's Style Making Aides Apprehensive," *The New York Times,* April 25, 1977, 61.
46. *Why Not the Best?,* pp. 9-12.
47. Gloria Spann, "Heartache of a Son," 63; Phyllis Battelle, "The Jimmy Carter's Untold Love Story," *Good Housekeeping* (October, 1976), 188.
48. Sally Quinn, "Behind the Grin of the Peanut Farmer from Georgia," *The Washington Post,* May 28, 1976 quoted in Wheeler, *Jimmy Who?,* p. 151.
49. Ibid.
50. Greider, "The Carter Years," *Journal-News* November 24, 1976, 6A, and November 25, 1976, 6A. See the story and photographs of Carter's Bull Sluice run in the *National Enquirer,* January 4, 1977, 1, 39; *The New York Times,* November 3, 1976; WINS Radio, January 2, 1977.
51. Battelle, "Untold Love Story," 188; *New York Daily News,* January 20, 1977, 56; Barbara Walters interview with Jimmy and Rosalynn Carter, *The Barbara Walters Special,* December 14, 1976, ABC-TV; "Playboy Interview: Jimmy Carter." *Playboy Magazine* (November, 1976), 74.
52. Gary Wills, "The Plains Truth: An Inquiry into the Shaping of Jimmy Carter," *The Atlantic Monthly* (June, 1976), 50; Gary Wills, "Carter On His Own," *The New York Review of Books* (November 25, 1976), 30.
53. *New York Daily News,* January 29, 1977, 6.
54. I am indebted to Lloyd deMause for sharing his methodology of Fantasy Analysis prior to the Institute for Psychohistory's Third Summer Workshop, August 2-4, 1977.

55. Barbara Walters interview with Jimmy and Rosalynn Carter.
56. *Why Not the Best?*, p. 22.
57. *The New York Times,* September 24, 1976, 1.
58. TRB, "Leap of Faith," *The New Republic* (May 8, 1976), 2.
59. *New York Daily News,* January 20, 1977, 31; Curtis, "What Kind of First Lady," 22; Sheehy, "Second President—Sister Rosalynn," 50.
60. Alex Haley, "President Jimmy Carter: I. From Boyhood on a Red-Dirt Farm to the Governorship of Georgia," *"A New Spirit, A New America": The Inauguration of President Jimmy Carter and Vice President Walter F. Mondale* (New York: Bantam Books, 1977), pp. 43-44.
61. Davis Newton Lott, *Jimmy Carter and How He Won* (Los Angeles: Peterson, 1976).
62. Interview with Delegate to the Democratic Convention, New York State Senator Robert Garcia, January 2, 1977.
63. "Playboy Interview," 66.
64. Walter Dean Burnham, "Jimmy Carter and the Democratic Crisis," *The New Republic,* (July 3 & 10, 1976), 19.
65. Jerald F. terHorst, *Gerald Ford and the Future of the Presidency* (New York: The Third Press, 1974). Bud Vestal, *Jerry Ford, Up Close: An Investigative Biography* (New York: Coward, McCann & Geoghegan, 1974). Richard Reeves, *A Ford, not a Lincoln* (New York and London: Harcourt Brace Jovanovich, 1975). When the psychohistory of Gerald Ford is undertaken, a major source will be the report of John Hersey's week-long stay with *The President* (New York: Alfred A. Knopf, 1975).
66. Rudolph Binion, *Hitler Among the Germans* (New York, Oxford and Amsterdam: Elsevier, 1976), p. 127.
67. *New York Daily News,* December 29, 1976, 3, 15: Roland Evans and Robert Novak, "Carter to City: 'Heal Thyself'," *New York Magazine* (March 14, 1976), 34-38.
68. Paul Monaco, "The Popular Cinema as Reflection of the Group Process in France, 1919-1929," *History of Childhood Quarterly: The Journal of Psychohistory* I (Spring, 1974), 607-635.
69. Simpson in *The Tulsa Tribune* reprinted in *Time Magazine* (February 28, 1977), 12.
70. Mazlish and Diamond, "Thrice-Born," 28-30.
71. John Weisman, "The Inauguration of Jimmy Carter," *TV Guide* (Local Programs, January 15-21, 1977), 5.
72. For a representative sampling of the work of Butler Brown see the photograph in *Newsweek,* January 24, 1977, 18. I am grateful to psychohistorian Paul Elovitz for the description of Carter's painting.
73. *Time,* January 3, 1977, 29.

CHAPTER FOUR

Carter and the Utopian Group-Fantasy

JOHN J.
HARTMAN

"When Democrats organize a firing squad they usually form a circle."[1] So said Morris Udall to the 1976 Democratic National Convention, declining nomination for president and urging his followers to support Jimmy Carter. Even before the convention, Democratic Chairman Robert Strauss assessed his party this way: "Anytime you got two Democrats in a room, they would form a steering committee to remove whoever was in power."[2] The factionalism, acrimony, and disarray of the Democrats when they gather in one place are infamous, well documented, and in recent years well-televised.[3] How was it, then, that in 1976 the Democrats achieved a unity and harmony unprecedented in their party's history? This unity was not simply in spirit. There were no major platform fights, no polarization of issues, and no rule disputes, despite many opportunities for these to occur. The party harmony generated by the convention is as much a political miracle as the success of the candidate himself. As Carter joked in his acceptance speech, unity among Democrats occurs only once every 200 years.[4]

This unity did not occur because it was necessary for victory. The Democrats have always needed unity to win. It did not come about solely because of the political skills of Robert Strauss or the sophistication of the delegates and caucuses. These have been available before. Harmony was not achieved because Carter had won the nomination and dominated the convention. If anything this might have tended to lead to revolt by anti-Carter forces on the platform, rules, or vice-presidency issues that were still up for grabs.

My view is that this unprecedented and surprising unity was a manifestation of a shared, unconscious, irrational utopian group-fantasy which evolved from the disastrous Democratic conventions and elections of 1968 and 1972. This fantasy derived its strength, too, from the national disasters associated with the Vietnam war, the Watergate scandals, and the resignation of a president. The ideology of the utopian group-fantasy derived from a desire for rebirth, revival, and a return to peace and security not only in the Democratic party but in the nation-as-a-whole. This fantasy found its focus and leader in Jimmy Carter whose personality, life experience, and philosophy embodied the fulfillment of these utopian wishes and ideals. The Carter campaign cleverly and intuitively grasped the fit between the utopian fantasy and their candidate's characteristics and utilized this knowledge effectively. Having experienced disasters, defeats, and suffering of various sorts, the Democrats and the country followed a process of group development well documented by group research—that of a desire for revitalization and rebirth through the creation of group unity and harmony. To symbolize this harmony and give it substance, a utopian hero—whose "born again" religious experience became such an issue—was perfectly suited to exemplify the peaceful rebirth of a divided Democratic party and of a troubled country on its birthday.

I shall try to amplify and document these assertions by drawing a comparison between the events of the Democratic National Convention and its historical context and the patterning of group development discovered in small group research.

GROUP DEVELOPMENT AND UTOPIAN FANTASIES

For the past 17 years I have been studying small face-to-face groups as a member, leader, or observer. These groups have met for educational or therapeutic purposes and have involved the study of the ongoing process and development within the groups themselves. Much has been written about these self-analysis groups.[5] Philip Slater has called them a "microcosm" of social processes.[6] Because of this experience and background, the atmosphere of the 1976 Democratic National Convention became quickly familiar to me. The unity was like that which I had seen develop so many times in small groups, a unity which many researchers had noted, and which Graham Gibbard and I had made a special focus in our previous work. A brief review of this work is in order here, but the reader is referred elsewhere for the details and evidence supporting these notions of group development.[7]

W. R. Bion,[8] a British psychoanalyst, argues that in every group there are two principal modes of functioning: "work" and "basic assumption" activity. Work in this context refers to a variety of rational, problem-solving endeavors (e.g., the attempt to analyze psychological phenomena). The basic assumptions, in contrast, are shared, unconscious fantasy constructions of the nature, purpose, and structure of the group. In the "dependency group" assumption, for example, the members act as if the group has assembled so that a single individual (usually the group leader) may protect and nurture the members. When the "fight-flight" assumption prevails, the group is characterized by frantic activity of one sort or another—an acting out of the fantasy that the group has met to fight and/or flee from someone or something. In a "pairing" group there is a tacit agreement that the purpose of the group is "pairing" and reproduction, to create a Messiah who will solve all the group's problems.

Bennis and Shepard[9] have offered a theory of group development which includes a phase characterized by a transfer of attention from problems of authority to problems of member-member intimacy. In this phase, a "myth of mutual acceptance and universal harmony" is present. There is a serious attempt to minimize hostility or competition and to establish solidarity, harmony, and love.

Dunphy,[10] in his study of myth in self-analytic groups, identifies a phase dominated by the hope for a "utopian group and a messiah hero." In this phase, which comes after a long period of "group paralysis" and depression, the group begins thinking about a "new dawning" and is concerned again about member-member friendship and intimacy. There is an effort to create an atmosphere of warmth, mutual understanding, and harmonious living, which Dunphy describes as a wish for an idealized group in which spontaneity, sharing, and cooperation exist.

Gibbard and I[11] have focused on these utopian fantasies and have related them to a theory of group development. The fantasy that the group is, or could become, a utopia reflects the emergence, at both an individual and a collective level, of deeply repressed psychological themes. More specifically, the utopian hopes are found to center on an aspect of the largely unconscious fantasy that the group-as-a-whole is a maternal entity, or some facet of such an entity. Acting on this fantasy, the group members seek to establish and maintain contact with "good," nurturant, and protective aspects of the group and to suppress or deny the existence of "bad," abandoning and destructive aspects of the group. The establishment of such a fantasied relationship appears to promise many positive gratifications. In addition, the fantasy offers some assurance that the more frightening, enveloping, or destructive aspects of the group-as-mother are held in check and that a host of frightening feelings will not become fully conscious and gain direct expression in the group.

The choice of the term *utopian* implies that the group members attempt to institute a state of affairs that is perfect or ideal, with conflict eliminated and replaced by a fantasy of unconditional and unlimited love, nurturance, and security. The utopian fantasy is more likely to appear when the positive and appealing aspects of the group-as-mother (warmth, security, protectiveness) seem to be attainable and the negative aspects (engulfment, malevolence, obliteration of self-object boundaries) appear to be well-defended against. The emergence of the fantasy is made possible by the individual's use of the mechanism of splitting, which allows him to maintain a consistent separation of good and bad and thus to avoid a state in which good and bad cannot be differentiated or a state in which both are experienced at the same time (genuine ambivalence).

We found that utopian fantasies typically emerged at specific times in the histories of our groups and played a particular role in development. When the groups were faced with great distress or were threatened with dissolution, a utopian fantasy aided in the re-establishment of cohesion and groupness. Rather than power struggles, sexual competition, or fears of disbanding, the utopian group experiences all obstacles to the Good Group as having been removed. There is then a direct effort to actualize this ideal conception.

We regard utopian group-fantasies as the product of a shared group regression to a form of relatedness characteristic of earlier childhood. On the individual level, Margaret Mahler has outlined stages of psychological development pre-dating the "psychological birth" of the infant.[12] She postulates a "symbiotic phase" in which the infant's view of self is indistinguishable from that of the mother. From this symbiosis the infant moves to psychological separation and individuation. We regard the utopian wish as analogous to the wish for a return to the unambivalent symbiosis of the early mother-child relationship.

We have also found that references to actual *biological birth* and to symbols of that event typically occur when utopian fantasies are present in the group. Why would references to and symbols of the biological birth process arise in relation to utopian fantasies and wishes in small groups? One answer is that it is a metaphoric expression of change, revival, and new life when these become necessary. There is no doubt about this function. Gibbard and I have postulated that the birth references are metaphoric, but this time symbolizing in more concrete form the psychological birth of "the self" in the separation-individuation developmental process as described by Mahler. As group development reflects individual development, group fantasies represent shared regressions to pre-individuation stages as in utopianism.

Recent work by Lloyd deMause[13] and Stanislav Grof[14] suggests another possibility. Their work suggests that group development manifests biological birth imagery because there is an actual *motivational causal nexus* between the experience of biological birth and group phenomena like wars, revolution, and utopianism. Seen in this light, the wish for change and rebirth in groups is dictated by a recapitulation of the actual birth process. Thus, the revolt-utopian sequence of group development would correspond in deMause's theory to an "upheaval" (revolt) and a return to a fantasy of nurturance, a new "Strong" condition (utopian).

While the work of deMause and Grof remains speculative and controversial, it has striking relevance to my work in small group research. Taken to its logical conclusion their work suggests that group development owes its nature and course to motives associated with both the biological as well as the psychological birth process.

Because we have regarded the small self-analytic group as a microcosm of social processes, Gibbard and I have drawn an analogy between our findings and utopian social movements. For example, the Ghost Dance Movement among the Plains Indians or the Cargo Cults of Melanesia are social movements which awaited the miraculous return to a Golden Age, ushered in by a messiah. The movements seemed to arise at times when the society in question was threatened with dissolution and extinction.

Michael Barkun,[15] a political scientist, has advanced a thesis concerning these utopian social movements which is in harmony with our group research. Barkun's thesis is that disasters and upheaval are the necessary, but not sufficient, conditions, for the emergence of utopian movements. Culture clash, economic depression, revolution, war, national catastrophes and other such disasters create a collective stress situation for a social group. Barkun concludes that when the individual loses his reference points to the most significant parts of his environment, that individual experiences anxiety, depression, and heightened suggestibility. Stress induced by disaster is thus a potent source for social change, as individuals seek ways to re-create significant reference points in a state of increased suggestibility. For Barkun, additional variables are necessary conditions for the appearance of a utopian movement as an antidote to this vulnerable condition: agrarian society, multiple disasters, the availability of a utopian ideology, and the presence of a potential charismatic leader.

Although based on a simplistic theory of psychological functioning, Barkun's work closely parallels our own findings in small groups. Utopian fantasies occur in these self-analytic groups in times of great stress and potential "disasters" for the group and its members.

Barkun's work has prompted the following thesis which can apply to all groups, large and small:

Utopian phenomena occur at those times in the group's history when its members share the belief, consciously or unconsciously, that the existing group basic assumption cannot or should not meet certain basic material and psychological needs because of some real or anticipated catastrophe. This belief produces in individuals a shared unconscious fantasy of psychological annihilation which harks back to the deepest anxieties of human development. The utopian beliefs can serve to cope with these deep anxieties and to produce another shared unconscious fantasy of fusion with an ideal mother, a recapitulation of feelings of earliest life, perhaps even *before* birth. To give life and meaning to the shared fantasy, the utopian group needs an ideology and a leader or it will decay and die.

If he is still with us on this journey, the reader is to be commended for putting up with our excursion into small group research and birth imagery. Unlike the infant in the birth canal, I have the impression that the reader knows all too well where we are heading—back to the "born-again convention" of 1976.

THE BORN-AGAIN CONVENTION

To restate my thesis: the success of the Carter campaign and the extraordinary unity of the Democratic Convention were products of a utopian group-fantasy generated by the party and national disasters of recent history. The Democrats and the country seized on a utopian ideology derived in part from fundamentalist Protestantism and found a suitable leader as mythic healer and symbol of rebirth.

The disasters of the Democrats in 1968 and 1972 were very real. In 1968 the incumbent President, Lyndon Johnson, decided not to seek re-election. The likeliest successor, Robert Kennedy, was killed. The Vietnam War deeply divided the party and the country. At the convention in Chicago, Democratic Mayor Richard Daley's police battled anti-war protesters and convention delegates alike. And the Democrats lost to Richard Nixon in November. In 1972, the liberals who lost out in 1968 took their turn and nominated George McGovern in Miami. This convention rivaled the last in its divisiveness and mismanagement. There were such battles over substantive issues in the party's platform and rules that McGovern's acceptance speech did not come until 3 a.m., hardly prime time. The vice-presidential nominee had to be removed because of a history of psychiatric treatment. Many Democrats would not support the McGovern campaign and a deeply divided party list by a "landslide." In 1968, polls before the convention showed Hubert Humphrey trailing Nixon by 6 percentage points. After the highly televised convention the margin became 15. In 1972 McGovern trailed Nixon by 12 points before and 23 after the convention. It is little wonder that political observers characterized these two conventions as "exciting disasters."[16]

It was not as if the country itself were smoothly sailing along either. The opposition to the war, city riots, bombings, escalations of the war were all a prelude to two national "disasters." The end of the Vietnam war marked a military and psychological defeat for the United States. The Watergate scandal ended with the resignation of the President. Both of these events were unprecedented. The mood and self-esteem of the country-as-a-whole had never been lower. The oil embargo added a further insult to a suffering nation. It was in this historical context that Gerald Ford became leader and Jimmy Carter decided to try to replace him.

These conditions were right, according to Michael Barkun's analysis, for utopian social movements to develop. We know, in fact, that a large number of pseudo-religious cults have gained thousands of adherents since 1972.[17] Some like the Unification Church of Rev. Sun Moon or the Children of God are messianic: others like Hare Krishna and the Divine Light Mission are based on Eastern teachings regarding inner utopia. Transcendental Meditation and various forms of exotic pseudo-therapies have appeared in this period also. Traditional religions have undergone a revival also. God is not dead. The wish for inner peace in a world of defeat, disillusionment, and discontent was the prevailing mood of the nation in the last five or so years.

The group-fantasy of the post-Nixon era involved a wish for a mythic healer to create a utopia of peace, security, unity, and harmony—to heal differences between liberal and conservative, black and white, rich and poor, male and female, North and South, pro-war and anti-war. What was needed was a unifier, not a polarizer. In this context it is not surprising that "nice-guy" Gerald Ford filled the role of healer. The contest between Ford and Carter could be seen as a test for the best healer and architect of a utopian group.

For the Democrats, the party had to be healed before the country. The person given that responsibility was Robert Strauss. Political writer Richard Reeves feels that the unity of the convention was due to 3½ years of dedicated effort by Strauss:

> He had become Democratic National Chairman on December 9, 1972, determined that, while he was in charge, his party would not meet in riot . . . or in fiasco . . . *"I'm not going to deliver a candidate to the party,"* he said that December. *"I'm going to deliver a party to the candidate . . . Medicine depends on what ails us and what medicine we need. We need a sedative."* If he had his way, the Democrats would be sedated—and Bob Strauss would scream, bully, bluff, charm, crawl, and lie a bit to make sure of it [italics mine].[18]

For his efforts Strauss has been hailed as a "miracle worker."[19] Interestingly Strauss chose Jimmy Carter to work as a liaison between the Democratic National Committee and the state parties. In 1974, a mini-convention was held in Kansas City. "We got out alive," Strauss observed.[20] A compromise on quotas for blacks and women for the 1976 convention was endorsed by both Barbara Jordan and Richard Daley. This was a harbinger of the unity to come. While I do not underestimate the skills of Strauss or the fact that Carter had the nomination "in the bag," the ultimate success of both was determined by the utopian group-fantasy. A healer was desperately sought and first one, then the other appeared.

During the convention week observers and delegates questioned whether the apparent unity and lack of dissent was "real." One explanation was that a combination of the rules that Strauss instituted to ensure a "smooth" convention along with the power of the Carter camp was able to stifle the real dissent present and thus create an illusion of harmony. By the end of the week it seemed clear to the political writers and the delegates, however, that the *feeling* of harmony and unity was real and that tangible signs of party unity were abundant. My view is that the mood and atmosphere of unity *was* real despite the obvious cleavages inherent in the Democratic coalition. These differences became submerged in the course of that week in the utopian group-fantasy. The strength of this fantasy produced significant tangible results.

What evidence do we have of this utopian group feeling? The evidence is the behavior during convention week itself and reactions to it. From the beginning, each day's events showed a building unity. One problem early in the week concerned the Women's Caucus' demand for 50% women at the next convention. This demand was not acceded to, only a compromise was written in the rules for a "goal" of 50% representation. Carter himself gave assurance of women at high levels in his administration, which satisfied the usually pugnacious women. The Black Caucus, likewise, went along with the consensus after being addressed by Carter, even though issues important to blacks were sidestepped in the platform. Representatives of war resisters and war veterans, hoping to remind Democrats of their part in the Vietnam war as well as future amnesty got little support. The anti-abortionists also failed to arouse much interest during the convention. Both issues were potentially explosive, but this was not the week for division or guilt. As I will argue later, it was not a week of killing babies but of producing them.

The convention became a ritual of harmony after the pockets of discontent were reassured. There were no battles over the party platform or rules. Twenty different people, representing diverse factions of the polygot Democratic party, from Richard Daley to Coretta Scott King, read parts of the platform, the past forgotten or forgiven. Udall, Wallace, Humphrey, and McGovern, all vocally and directly (if not enthusiastically) urged support of Carter. Even the fact that there were fewer blacks and women at the convention than in 1972, and that there were no guarantees that this would change in 1980 caused no discontent. The greatest interest of the convention, the choice of liberal, Humphrey-protegee Walter Mondale as vice-president, caused few ripples of dissent either. Edward Kennedy seemed to pout and did not attend Carter's acceptance speech, but no one seemed to care. Jerry Brown, a genuine utopian himself, was the last opposition to join the united front, but his reluctance made him look foolish rather than heroic.

The imagery of the convention as captured by articles in the *New York Times* during convention week is decidedly utopian: "Pervasive atmosphere of sweetness and light," "rhetoric of unity and God," "Democratic harmony," "four days in a sea of good will," "orgy of togetherness," "less a convention than a festival."[21] Finally James Naughton of the *Times* summarized the convention this way:

> Mr. Carter and his running mate, Senator Walter F. Mondale of
> of Minnesota, now face the larger task of persuading the nation
> that there is substance to their promise of a new millenium. . .[22]

The convention itself gave some credence to the idea that the millenium had already arrived, and in New York City of all places. Radicals Tom Hayden and Jane Fonda, veterans of civil-rights and Vietnam protests, had nothing bad to say about Jimmy Carter on national television. George Wallace shook hands with Martin Luther King, Sr. The Mississippi delegation was the most sexually and racially integrated on the floor. Aaron Henry, head of the NAACP in the turbulent 50's, and Ross Barnett, Jr., son of the governor during the Ole Miss riots, were both delegates and hugged in a show of unity. This "festival of harmony" went on all week. Reeves' account, as well as that of the *New York Times,* suggests that this utopian mood was so strong that it spread into New York City itself. The city was on its best behavior, crime was down, and prostitutes under control for that week. But there were more astounding events. Good samaritan New York citizens went out of their way to find lost children, policemen politely gave directions, and a cabby refused a tip![23] Miracles abounded in and out of the convention.

The week culminated in Mondale's and Carter's acceptance speeches, after which all the party leaders trooped to the stage. A rousing benediction by Martin Luther King, Sr., and the singing of "We Shall Overcome," gave emotional reality to the unity and harmony of the convention. The utopian group-fantasy had produced a mythic healer. It also produced some tangible results. Jimmy Carter led Gerald Ford by 13 percentage points before and by 39 points just after the convention.[24] Needless to say, the unity of the convention helped to elect the first Democratic president since 1964.

The unity of this Democratic convention was called "strange" and "surprising," and was hard to explain for political scientists and political observers generally.[25] Some attributed it to the Democrats' desire to win above all else and to the likelihood of that victory, some to the dominance of the Carter campaign and the skills of Robert Strauss. Still others analyzed the convention's unity as a product of a complicated series of negotiations and accommodations. Group developmental theory offers not an alternative but a deepening of these explanations based on a particular view of individual psychology and the influence of unconscious shared perceptions and motivations. Politicians negotiate, plan, accommodate, and maneuver. But like all of us, they can come under the influence of group-fantasies which pull on buried emotions from the distant past.

The ideology which gave the utopian hopes substance and form was based on an unlikely mixture of "Winning Through Team Play" and fundamentalist Protestant Christianity. The latter particularly with its emphasis on the *experience* of personal rebirth, emotionality, and disdain of ritual provided a suitable rationale for the harmony of the convention and the translation of Christian love into political life. The convention became more and more like a Baptist revival meeting until finally Mondale, Carter, and Rev. King climaxed the emotional experience of party harmony. This evangelical tradition has not always had such an impact on our politics but it seems ideally suited for 1976.[26]

It is entirely consistent with this view that a party seeking revitalization, if not rebirth, would find in its ranks someone who could symbolize this evangelical, utopian "born again" ideology. Carter, by virtue of his Southern Baptist background and his personal rebirth experience in 1966 (after his defeat for governor), would seem ideally suited for such a role. Just as Christianity became a revitalization movement of Judaism by fulfilling the messianic hope, so the Carter campaign gave substance to the political rebirth of the Democratic party. This imagery was even used by delegates who had placards depicting Jimmy Carter as Jesus Christ. Carter was referred to by his staff and by his detractors as J.C. If in this fantasy Carter was the messiah-hero, Robert Strauss, a Texas Jew, was certainly John the Baptist!

Not only background and ideology but also his personality fitted Jimmy Carter for his role as mythic healer. His complicated personal makeup and, yes, his "fuzziness" on issues, allowed him to be many contradictory things to many diverse people. Carter is a unifier, not a polarizer. He is a liberal and a conservative, he is a scientist and a humanist, he is gentle and tough, he is outstanding and ordinary. These contradictions abound in Carter, yet seem unified in a self-confident, planful, ambitious identity. By personal example Carter has seemed to master the essential dilemmas of our times—relations between the sexes, relations between the races, modern technology, personal identity and roots, relations between the individual and large impersonal institutions. He is the small, individualistic farmer who made it big and can control the monstrous federal government. He is a white man who has the respect and friendship of blacks. He sews his own clothes, fixes his own breakfast, has an ongoing marriage and has raised apparently normal children. To top is off he is an "expert" on the most dangerous of modern problems—nuclear energy.

Jimmy Carter's role as healer is strengthened by his mastery of these problems in his own life. The healing tradition comes from his mother who was the community nurse, a tradition given different form by his faith-healing sister, Ruth Stapleton. There are marked "feminine" traits of nurturing, healing, and gentleness which combine with his more traditionally "masculine" military toughness, planning, and ambitiousness to make Carter a complex but integrated personality.

THE BIRTH OF THE HERO

I mentioned earlier that my small group research with Graham Gibbard revealed that imagery connected directly or symbolically with the biological birth typically accompanied the utopian group fantasy. If the thesis of this paper is correct, we would expect to find evidence of such imagery in the Democratic Convention. This kind of birth imagery would relate to a peaceful, harmonious oneness with the mother, a fusion in the Good Womb.

Robert Strauss seemed to be dimly aware of this birth-rebirth fantasy in the earlier quoted assessment of his role. He was going to "deliver a party to the candidate," and to do so with a "sedative." While one does deliver votes, one also delivers babies. The word *deliver* is derived from the Latin, meaning "to free from." Just as Strauss was going to free the Democrats from the suffering catastrophes of the past, so the obstetrician frees the struggling infant from the pressures, dangers, and suffering of the birth canal. If Strauss unconsciously saw himself as the obstetrician for the rebirth of the Democratic party, he seemed to be offering a painless delivery. To carry this analogy further, the convention "body" as-a-whole becomes in fantasy the mother's womb and the candidate becomes the heroic-messiah-baby, symbolic of hope and rebirth. Mondale observed in his acceptance speech: "Carter is the embodiment of hope and the dream not only of Democrats but of all Americans."[27] That everything about this convention seemed so "miraculous," including the candidate's rapid rise from obscurity, and the unity of the party, further reinforces the birth motif. Birth is a miracle, especially the birth of a messiah.

Symbols of the birth process in dreams and myths often involve bodies of water and boats.[28] A calm and tranquil sea represents the amniotic fluid in the Good Womb. A flood or waves represent the envelopment and dangers of the birth process. This imagery was evident in the acceptance speeches and in the reporting of the events of the convention. The convention itself was characterized as "four days in a sea of good will, mostly."[29] There were constant references to not wanting to "make waves" or "rock the boat." Mondale cited the past "waves of division [which] swept over us"[30] in previous conventions.

There is another symbol, darkness and blazing light, which has significance for the birth process also. The darkness of the birth canal gives way to the "light at the end of the tunnel." Mondale seemed fond of this imagery, too, in his acceptance speech. He talked about "the healing sunshine," and went on to quote Carl Sandberg's vision of:

An America, not in the *setting sun* of a *black night with despair ahead of us* but an America in the *crimson light* of a *rising sun* fresh from the *burning creative* hand of God [italics mine].[31]

This seems to be an image of birth and constant renewal, the utopian hope.

One might argue that birth imagery is so appropriate on the 200th birthday of the nation, that making so much of it psychologically is stretching a metaphor unnecessarily. The rebirth motif was so pervasive not only in specific language, however, but in the whole process and emotional mood of the convention to sustain this interpretation.

The highlight of the convention was the appearance of the presidential candidate and his acceptance speech. In this case the staging of that particular event seems to have been artistically, even inspirationally, done. The original plan was to have Carter appear suddenly in a spotlight after the showing of his campaign film. At the last minute, Jerry Rafshoon hit upon the idea that Carter should enter from the rear of the hall and walk through the delegates to the podium.[32] This decision seems to me to have been a creative act involving an appreciation of the underlying fantasies of the delegates. By having Carter enter from the rear of the building it gave the impression that Carter stepped out of the film which depicted his origins and into the leadership of the party. This was to symbolize in Rafshoon's mind that Carter came from the people rather than the manipulative party bosses, unseen in the background. In the light of the utopian fantasy and the birth imagery that accompanies it, it would seem that in addition Carter's coming through the body of delegates symbolized that he was born through the loins of the delegates themselves to become the infant messiah of the Democratic party.

Carter, himself, seemed particularly in tune with the birth motif of the

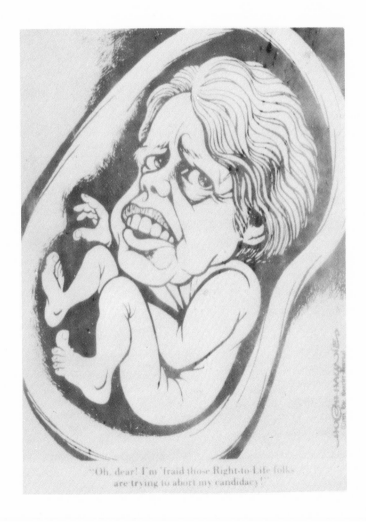

Illustration 1— This cartoon directly portrays Carter as a fetus. Because the utopian group-fantasy had not been completely accepted, he is seen as danger.

"WELCOME ABOARD, FRITZ!"

Illustration 2— This cartoon portrays two group-fantasy themes. The first is Carter's Christ-like ability to walk on water. The second is the portrayal of the campaign as a tranquil sea, symbolic of the Good Womb.

Why Carter Won't Be The Savior We Expected

Illustration 3— By March of 1977, the utopian group-fantasy is beginning to decay. In this magazine cover Carter is depicted as holy but the caption warns against expecting too much.

Illustration 4— This cartoon illustrates the point that Carter's evangelical ideology was taken on by the Democratic party as a whole. It also illustrates that such an ideology triumphs over the ''deathly'' rivalry and bitterness which had lately affected the Democrats but which is now a Republican problem. The Utopian group-fantasy emerges from feelings of death and dissolution.

utopian group-fantasy. His acceptance speech is replete with birth imagery. His characterizations of the failures of the recent past which his administration would "heal" were characterized by such metaphors as: "decay," "crippled," "adrift," "torment," "suffering," "tight secrecy," "bloated bureaucracy," "unwarranted pressures." One could read this suffering as analogous to that of the birth process. The solution, Carter went on to say, lies in "going back" to the basic values of America's birth and to the solutions of the Democratic party in its more glorious past. This Golden Age for both Mondale and Carter was Franklin Roosevelt's administration, although homage was paid to Harry Truman, John Kennedy, and even Lyndon Johnson. Carter's metaphor included a quote from Bob Dylan stressing Mondale's point again: "America is busy being born, not busy dying."[33] This is a fantasy of America in continual rebirth, and not decay. This is an especially appealing metaphor for a country which had just experienced its first military defeat, its first resignation by a president, and other insults and calamities. The utopian wish for rebirth is strongest in despair, with the threat of group decay and dissolution.

Jimmy Carter's own experience of his entry into the hall for his speech is very revealing also. The *New York Times* article on Carter the day after the nomination records the candidate's emotional experience:

> After saying that at his nomination last night he had experienced "as highly emotional a feeling as I've ever had," Mr. Carter, who always seems cool and controlled, described his sensations as *"a feeling of a cocoon"*—I just felt kind of *surrounded* by friends and *protected*. I am not easily overwhelmed and it was something we had anticipated, obviously not a surprise," he said. "But I was surprised at the intensity of my feeling when I walked into the hall. I hadn't seen it before. I had just seen it through the television lens—the number of people there and the *tightness* of it, the sense of friendship toward me, the acceptability, the harmony" (italics mine).[34]

The tight, surrounded, protected feeling of a cocoon that Carter describes is the feeling of fusion between the fetus and the Good Womb. This moment marks the culmination of the utopian group-fantasy, the return to the safety and protection of fusion and unity with the mother. It represents a union with the ideal Democratic party as well.

CONCLUSION

The harmonious feelings created by the convention certainly helped

Carter's popularity with the country directly afterwards. The utopian group-fantasy faded by November when his margin over Ford was considerably reduced. Doubts about Carter clouded the utopian fantasy and Ford was a unifier and a healer in his own right. But Carter did win the election and at this writing enjoys tremendous popularity in the country. His ability to appeal to unity and harmony has not yet worn off.

This analysis is not meant to suggest that Carter himself is a utopian in his approach to solving problems. It is another one of those seeming contradictions in his personality that a strong idealism and faith is harnessed to a practical, efficient engineer's desire to solve problems competently and efficiently. In his campaign rhetoric Carter said he wanted to translate love into practical day-to-day, competent government. In accomplishing this Carter must become the leader of the work-group, that rational problem-solving function which has as its goal the fulfillment of the group's primary task. In this effort Carter will be opposed by the tendency in all of us to wish him to be the messiah-hero, the mythic healer of the group-fantasy. We will wish him to be the miracle worker who will solve all the tough problems without asking us for work, self-sacrifice, and temporary goals.

Carter's task ahead is to harness the hope, unity, and confidence bred of the group-fantasy to accomplish realistic goals in the areas of energy, economy, health care, etc. necessary to our well-being. He must use the optimism and idealism renewed in the country to sustain us in the work ahead. The danger lies in the fact that the utopian-group-fantasy inevitably clashes with the political, economic, and psychological realities of power, scarcity, competition, and division. A fantasy is a fantasy, after all, and reality catches up with us sooner or later. If Carter is not able to translate the ideals into practical actions, the potential for disillusionment, disappointment, and subsequent rage is very great. For example, *New York Magazine* recently ran a story with the sub-title, "Why Carter won't be the savior we expected."[35] It was accompanied by a cartoon showing Carter on a small island with large waves mounting around him. While the utopian group-fantasy is instrumental in establishing group cohesion, solidarity, and hope its precipitous decay can lead to danger. Carter seems fully aware of this possibility and his ability to sustain the country's cooperation and optimism in solving its real problems will be the true test of his greatness. As a citizen and participant in the accomplishment of the country's goals, I'm betting on Jimmy Carter. As a psychohistorian, I am a little worried.

John J. Hartman, PhD, is Associate Professor of Psychology in the De-partment of Psychiatry at the University of Michigan and Director of the Group Relations Study Project there. He is a Research Associate of the Institute for Psychohistory and has written extensively on developmental processes in small groups, and is co-editor of Analysis of Groups. *He became a supporter of Jimmy Carter in the spring of 1976 and remains so.*

REFERENCES

1. *New York Times,* July 16, 1976, p. 14.
2. Greenfield, M. "The Miracle Worker," *Newsweek,* July 19, 1976, p. 80.
3. See, for example, Miller, A.H. Miller, W.E., Raine, A.S. and Brown, T.A. "A Majority Party in Disarray: Policy Polarization in the 1972 Election." Presented at the Annual Meeting of the American Political Science Association, New Orleans, 1973. Sullivan, D.G., Pressman, J.L., Page, B.I., and Lyons, J.J. *The Politics of Representation: The Democratic Convention 1972,* St. Martin's Press, New York, 1974.
4. *New York Times,* July 16, 1976, p. 10.
5. See for example Gibbard, G.S., Hartman, J.J. and Mann, R.D., Eds. *Analysis of Groups,* Jossey-Bass, San Francisco, 1974; Mann, R.D. *Interpersonal Styles and Group Development,* Wiley, New York, 1967.
6. Slater, P.E. *Microcosm,* Wiley, New York, 1966.
7. See especially *Analysis of Groups, op. cit.,* Chapters 7, 10, 13; Gibbard, G.S., and Hartman, J.J., "The Significance of Utopian Fantasies in Small Groups," *International Journal of Group Psychotherapy,* XXIII (1973) pp. 125-147; Hartman and Gibbard, "The Bisexual Fantasy and Group process," *Contemporary Psychoanalysis* IX (1973), pp. 303-322.
8. Bion, W.R. *Experiences in Groups,* Basic Books, New York, 1959.
9. Bennis, W.G., and Shepard, H.A. "A Theory of Group development," *Human Relations,* IX (1956), pp. 415-437.
10. Dunphy, D.C. "Phases, Roles, and Myths in Self-Analytic Groups," *Journal of Applied Behavioral Science,* IV (1968), pp. 195-225.
11. See note 7.
12. Mahler, M.S., Pine, F., and Bergman, A. *The Psychological Birth of the Human Infant: Symbiosis and Individuation,* Basic Books, New York, 1975.
13. deMause, L. "The Independence of Psychohistory." In *The New Psychohistory* (Lloyd deMause, Ed.) The Psychohistory Press, New York, 1975. de Mause, L. "The Formation of the American Personality Through Psychospeciation" *This Journal* IV (1976), 1-30. de Mause, L. "The Psychogenic Theory of History" IV (1977) pp. 253-267. de Mause, L. Chapter 1 of this book.

14. Grof, S. "Perinatal Roots of Wars, Totalitarianism, and Revolutions," *Journal of Psychohistory,* IV (1977), pp. 269-308.
15. Barkun, M. *Disaster and the Millenium,* Yale University Press, New Haven, 1974.
16. Reeves, R. *Convention,* Harcourt, Brace, Jovanovich, 1977, p. 220.
17. See for example Patrick, T. *Let Our Children Go,* E.P. Dutton, New York, 1976.
18. Reeves, *op. cit.,* p. 7.
19. Greenfield, *op. cit.*
20. *Ibid.*
21. *New York Times,* July 14, 15, 16, 17, 1976.
22. Naughton, J. "Democratic Harmony," *New York Times,* July 17, 1976, p. 7.
23. See Reeves, *op. cit.,* as well as *New York Times,* July 14, 15, 16, 1976.
24. Reeves, *op. cit.,* p. 220.
25. Sullivan, D.G., Pressman, J.L., Arterton, F.C., Nakamura, R.T., Weinberg, M.W. "Candidates, Caucuses, and Issues: The Democratic Convention 1976." Paper presented to American Political Science Association, Chicago, September 1976.
26. For a discussion of this point see Wills, G. "Love and Profit," *New York Review of Books,* August 5, 1976, pp. 17-21. Hardwick, E. "Piety and Politics," *New York Review of Books,* August 5, 1976, pp. 22, 27-28.
27. *New York Times,* July 16, 1976, p. 10.
28. See Freud, S. *The Interpretation of Dreams. Standard Edition,* Vols. 4, 5, Hogarth, London, 1953. Ferenczi, S. *Thalassa: A Theory of Genitality,* Norton, New York, 1968. Fodor, N. *The Search for the Beloved,* University Books, New Hyde Park, 1949.
29. *New York Times,* July 14, 1976, p. 24.
30. *New York Times,* July 16, 1976, p. 10.
31. *ibid.*
32. *New York Times,* July 17, 1976, p. 7.
33. *New York Times,* July 16, 1976, p. 10.
34. *New York Times,* July 17, 1976, p. 7.
35. Evans, R. and Novak, R. "Carter to City: Heal Thyself," *New York Magazine,* March 14, 1977, pp. 34-38.

CHAPTER FIVE

But What Kind of Baby is Jimmy Carter?

HENRY EBEL

The President, Führer, Generalissimo, Imperator is the *most* biggest grown-up in the entire country. He is a "father figure," the incarnation of potency, and we seldom see him—or his statues, portraits, and photographs—except in raised positions that confirm us in our sense of childlike inferiority to so ostentatious a presence. Since he is Numero Uno, Big Boss, or First Citizen, it seems natural enough—rational, inevitable, perfectly appropriate—that our gossip, our newspapers and our TV programs should be obsessively concerned with the minutest details of his policies, family life, habits, and personal appearance.

But the President, Führer, Generalissimo, Imperator is also our biggest and most infinitely precious baby. The radiating networks of assistants, executioners and flunkies that testify to the potency of his word can be read, easily enough, as life support systems. Unless he absolutely insists on doing so, the leader is the man who never needs to open a door or drive a car or sign a check or carry his own clothes, and whose almost "feminine" fragility needs a staff of thousands to protect it. Even when he is in the terminal stages of senility or corruption, great pains are taken—quite spontaneously—to keep from hurting his feelings. The taxi driver who calls you or me a rotten motherfucker for getting in his way is just expressing the understandable exasperation of urban life, but the man who puts the same words on a placard and carries them up and down in front of the White House is felt to be in very bad taste—like Galahad suddenly giving Guinevere a belt in the kisser, or like a grown man choosing to terrorize a vulnerable, open-eyed little boy.

The leader is sacred and unattainable, so that even a few minutes spent in his august presence constitute a reason for boasting, and a phone call from him—if we are not among those in regular attendance on his person—can easily become the subject of a newspaper article. But when the same newspapers discuss his family's presence in the national mansion reserved for his use, it is usually in terms—and tones—drawn from Winnie the Pooh. Whether he is Boston Irish rich in his origins or Georgia middle class, the appropriate affect for the new resident is ingenuous, wide-eyed eagerness, an "isn't-it-all-too-amazing" cuteness that seems to ellide the difference between the leader and his children, and that is imposed even when the people in question are rich, sophisticated, competent, or hard-bitten.

And sometimes the childlike quality of the supreme leader becomes even more explicit. The keepers of the infant Louis XIII seemed to regard him as a ferociously sexed rapist who wanted everyone at court to kiss his penis. In turn, his own offspring, the Sun King, received his courtiers every morning in an oversized crib, and discussed state issues with them while sitting on the potty. Churchill, when not striking a bulldog pose, looked like an overgrown chubby baby. He often wore an outfit oddly reminiscent of an infant's one-piece pajama suit, had to be kept supplied with palliatives like brandy and cigars if he was not to fall into a vile temper, and in his declining years was repeatedly photographed with his wife in the position of a dependent—with her arm covering his, in the posture traditional to husbands-and-wives and parents-and-children. Franklin Roosevelt—and JFK, in his own way—was a cripple. The rocking-chair, like the wheel-chair, is associated with weakness and dependency. The former is often given to children and the elderly; the latter is strikingly reminiscent of an infant's stroller.

And all supreme leaders are expected to have something about them that is playful and childishly appealing: Roosevelt and his stamp collection, Harry Truman banging away at the piano, Eisenhower playing golf, Kennedy on a sailboat, Hitler and his passion for creamy cakes . . . some quality, or harmless fetishism, that is suggestive of a "real and little" man behind the magnified image, and which suggests even more specifically a harmless *child* who is only role-playing at the office he has been saddled with. Hitler's sweet tooth was concealed from the public, of course; but for outside display he had that weird, glow-eyed, almost impish smile that made the knees of the German *Hausfrau* go weak with adoration, and had any of his female adorers gotten her hands on him a plate of pastry would have made its appearance forthwith. Elizabeth the First was so ruthlessly retarded that she banished all married people from her court, and created an erotic preserve whose sublimations and denials gave it a pre-pubescent or "latency" character. Nor did the grim shadow of Tudor despotism forbid her from being painted in the very act of doing the Lavolta, a dance that required its participants to leap (apparently) three or four feet into the air. The decadent amusements of Tiberius were not considered sufficient grounds for assassination or removal, and sexual scandals associated with politicians of the highest rank are first denied and suppressed, on the grounds that nothing less than a kittenish innocence is compatible with the highest of offices, and then (if espionage or death are not involved) taken with remarkable calmness, on the grounds that harmless erotic regressions are only to be expected from a representative of the Nation.

But the most infantile fact about the President, Führer, Generalissimo, Imperator is the fact that he is so very *there*. Right *there,* in the very Center of things. The rage for centralization that produced the nation-states of Europe and the rest of the globe out of tribal and regional constituencies—and whose limitations and irrationalities we are becoming painfully aware of—seemed also to require an absolute centralized capital, in the center or vicinity of which was one building that would henceforth serve as berth, cocoon, and *locus operandi* for Him (or, sometimes, Her)—though its externals could differ in detail from the homeliness of Ten Downing Street to the impenetrability of the Kremlin and the grandeur of Versailles. And around the really-not-very-promising medieval institution of kingship was woven the aura of mystical *thereness* that has clung to the highest office ever since.

Now, the outstanding fact about a newborn child is the quality of self-involvement and self-concern that is sometimes labelled "primary narcissism," and even a child of two is still blissfully unaware that by hitting you in the head as hard as he can with his favorite wooden toy he is actually causing you hurt. What makes young children so uniquely charming is this quality of self-involvement or self-absorption, the ability to remain unaware of the implicit demands that "others" make for a highly formalized, socialized persona—for the mask of tact and deference that we try to claw away (mostly without success) in our therapeutic thrashings. And it requires no great leap of the imagination to see this infantile quality not as the mere absence of socialization but as the natural continuation of the complete trancelike centrality that the fetus enjoyed in the womb, the only life support system of which we can ever say that it was wholly, unchallengeably our own.

The President, Führer, Generalissimo, Imperator is the projective re-creation of this really nonreproducible state of affairs. As he glides past us, and we feel ourselves "turn on" in the vast throng lining the streets, he smiles at no one in particular, feeling himself in the embrace of so vast and undifferentiated a hug, an outpouring aimed so completely and centrally at *him*. And we in turn, feeling in our bones the pleasure he is having in our adoration—and it hardly matters at this point whether he is Hitler, or JFK, or Ringo Starr—give those squeals and smiles of pleasure that belong, in their origin, to the world of little babies. The occasion is numinous. It crackles with electricity.

But there is yet another aspect of the *maximo lider's* infantile quality, a particularly dynamic one concerned, ultimately, with the birth process itself. When we elect or select our first and most important citizen, we ordinarily say he is going to fill a position or an "office"—which is patently inadequate, since an office is nothing but a segment of geography, while the leader, as our newspapers testify daily, is particularly involved in functioning over *time*. In fact, he is our delegate in seeking to cope with the great and infinitely unexpected unknown called the Future, and his life, once he is in "office," is totally bound up with "crises," "developments," "contingencies," and "plans."

What, then, are we electing him *for*? And how is it possible to pull a lever, or otherwise register assent, for a person who must cope—possibly with competence, and possibly disastrously—with that-which-we-know-nothing-about? What vision of functioning, however subliminal, is in our minds as we go through our end of the "political process"?

All of us, I think, have a very clear notion of what we are electing our leader to do, even if we cannot specify a single concrete context in which he will actually be doing it. We elect a leader (or otherwise assent in his taking power) so that he will be *under pressure,* relentlessly exposed to the "demands of office," on call day and night for a ceaseless stream of demands and emergencies . . . not to mention a daily torrent of meetings, memoranda, reports, entreaties, phone calls, complaints, requirements, plane trips and conferences. And at the same time that he is exposed to this superhuman burden of high-intensity pressure, we know that he will be clinically observed by a hundred newspapers, a thousand columnists, all the networks, and most of the world's population—all waiting breathlessly for him to make a boo-boo, fall down a flight of stairs, offend the Russians, go impotent on his wife, or otherwise crack under the strain. And whether his slips are excused, villified, tolerated or loved, the common denominator of his life, as he struggles with his nightmarishly huge responsibilities, will be the particular nightmare of having his struggles *watched.*

As we grope through the repertoire of human experience for some analogy to these characteristics of high office, there is one and one alone that fits the bill. You or I are struggling to be born, experiencing the titanic upheavals of the birth canal, and literally "struggling forward into our future." Indeed, this earliest and most tumultuous of all our journeys is a unique "synaesthesia" of time and space, and probably lays the foundation for all the later concerns—whether in an individual career or a millenarian movement—expressed in such metaphors as "moving forward into the future," "climbing the achievement ladder," "inching toward the goal." (If we were all caesarean babies, would anyone play, or watch, football?) And when we have gotten ourselves through the tunnel, we find—in the bad old world that preceded (and in most cases still precedes) Frederick Leboyer—that the nightmare has only begun. Our source of oxygen is almost instantaneously hacked away, and we find ourselves struggling to breathe. The temperature undergoes a violent drop, and we find ourselves struggling for warmth. Our backbone is abruptly, hideously stretched, and we find ourselves struggling with the pain of a new and premature posture. Above all, we find ourselves struggling to cope with the trauma that these obstetric disasters reinforce, the separation from our ancestral home, from the warm hearth of our earliest childhood. And all the while we are being *stared* at by clinical eyes surmounting clinical masks, and by the great glaring eye of a high-intensity light.

The experience is oddly similar to Arthur Koestler's description of the 1930's, when the victim of Nazi persecution found the rest of the world weirdly indifferent to his sufferings—as if, Koestler wrote, a man were being beaten to death within sight of a suburban railway platform, and the commuters seemed not to *hear* his anguished screams, and simply went on reading their newspapers. But perhaps even the events of the 1930's were a replay of the primal drama that we impose, in so many ways, on Presidents, Führers, Generalissimos, and Imperators.

If Frederick Leboyer is right (and a mountain of evidence, steadily growing, suggests that he is), then we are primally the recipients of a gratuitous act of aggression that must leave us with a great deal of anger. And since that aggression is imposed at a time when we are uniquely incapable of striking back, all of it must be turned inward, leaving us with the masochistic endowment that seems so universal to our species and that has puzzled our best minds long before and for some time after the career of Sigmund Freud. Later, when our powers are more highly developed, we might be expected to turn that anger outward again, but in contexts that recall—at least unconsciously—the original circumstances in which it was generated.

And indeed, once we have acknowledged the elements of odd over-protectiveness that are lavished on our highest leaders, the cherishing of our projective baby as a uniquely frail and precious object, we must also do justice to the elements of malice that underlie this most ambivalent of relationships. How we relish the frailties of the *maximo lider,* how we gloat over the fall of princes! We acquiesce in the perquisites of office because almost no reward seems too great for the One delegated to relive the pressures of birth, the toothpaste-tube squeeze that carries us to our future. And at the same time we acquiesce with secret enthusiasm in the group resentment that seeks to spoil, by probing and prying, every element of privacy and spontaneity that the poor schlepp might seek to retain during his years in office. And if by any chance he commits the supreme blunder à la Nixon or Teddy Kennedy, we give carte blanche to our bloodhounds the Press to dissect his every twitch and tremble, to poke at his mask of dignity until he resembles nothing so much as a tearful, humiliated child who has proven incompetent, and whose poo-poos are streaming publicly, disastrously, down his legs . . . or, in the earlier humiliation on which all later ones build, a ghastly bloodstained fetus getting his illcome into the horror called Life.

In short, the relationship we have to our leaders makes conventional notions of "ambivalence" seem understated and inadequate. The projections we pour into him or her are the truly primal ones that have to do with our initial infantile splittings between narcissistic self-adoration and apocalyptic self-loathing. In turn, the severity of the splitting can be traced to the deficits in the gratification of infantile needs that have historically been the norm for our species. The newborn *needs* a pain-free and nurturing environment, and an exceptional attentiveness on the part of its guardians (particularly, of course, its mother) if it is ever to achieve the transition from the literally self-centered womb—in which desire and gratification were nearly synchronous—to a world of delays inhabited by other needful and therefore competitive human beings. And it is therefore disastrous when, as has historically been the case, the needed attentiveness itself takes a painful form, in which swaddling, ritual mutilation, bottle-feeding, or obsessive cleanliness take the place of warmth, eye-contact, play, and the breast. The result is a cognitive bad connection from which none of us is wholly free: the fact that we feed on attention and have a truly awesome hunger for publicity, fame, and personal exposure—that even a dry letter informing us that we have won a prize or gotten an article accepted for publication is capable of sending a charge of infantile bliss through our systems—while feeling at the same time that no amount of admiration and achievement is "enough," and that our true position in life is that of a brutally and unfairly deprived innocent. Thus our victories in life are contaminated by the feeling that we are bad and don't deserve them, while our disasters are resented as the unjust persecution of a good baby who deserves better!

Perhaps it is now somewhat clearer why the job of *maximo lider* is such a dangerous one. It moves, has always moved, and *will* always move—with no rest in between—from the pole of untrammeled bliss to the pole of assassination and degradation. And close attention is needed to the dynamics we too often take for granted if we are to understand why this is so. Like the infant struggling with the paradoxes of birth, like the "adult" struggling with the good-baby/bad-baby voices that goad him through life, the leader is the allegorical and supremely concentrated expression of our magical relationship, as individuals, to time and vicissitude. We never get over our initial discovery—which might be termed philosophy written in fire—that no condition endures, and that built into the nature of things is a continuous, tragic, irreparable, and ongoing separation from our pasts. The only exception to the rule is provided by experiences so complete and fulfilling that they can be internalized as a "permanent present" in our personalities, a neurological layer that transmits feelings of stability and security even in the midst of danger and dislocation—experiences represented, above all, by the incomparable blisses of handling and feeding in infancy. Since it is precisely these experiences that have been short-circuited or eliminated by our customary practices in child-rearing, we have spent most of our collective and individual lives in brooding over the Fall of Man, and in creating a role called "leader" that enables us to contain, through projection, the pain-inducing fact that our titanic infantile strivings took us ever further from Eden, ever deeper into Death Valley. It is certainly no accident that a religion of loss and regret like Christianity also produced the incomparable image of the Wheel of Fortune, on whose rotating spokes the kings and princes of the world move inexorably from humble beginnings to triumph and disaster.

All of which is perfectly clear, and yet almost impossible to believe, especially when we focus our attention on the leader who *currently* serves the demands of our collectivized fantasy. When one considers how hard he works, how many papers he studies and signs, and the awesome power of the red buttons he controls, it is difficult to accept the notion that Jimmy Carter's primary overriding function, in the minds of the individuals who elected him and whom he "rules," is that of an infantile projection. At best we might feel willing to admit that the objective and rational aspects of the presidential office are accompanied by an overlay or admixture of irrationalities and projections. After all, don't we need *some* controlling figure to cope with the aspects of reality that have nothing to do with our inner fantasies—the floods, earthquakes, shortages, and aggressions which are "out there" and in no sense part of ourselves?

It is extremely interesting in this connection that the leaders in earlier historical periods, whose functioning was rationalized in precisely these terms, are so much easier for us to "see through." Churchill and Roosevelt, for example, must have known in a matter of months that German war production was rising despite the unprecedented quantities of bombs being unleashed by the Allies, and that the bombings were providing the trump card in Goebbels' propaganda. The fact that they could not stop themselves—and even more grotesquely, that their error was repeated under even less favorable circumstances two decades later—had nothing to do with even the crudest notions of rationality, and had everything to do with infantile rage. (It seems to be documented truth, for example, that Churchill was "sold" on the bombing campaign by a special Walt Disney film featuring the lovable cartoon characters with whom we are all familiar.) And the fact that *we*—and not their contemporaries—are the ones who can "see through" them has everything to do with the fact that a leader's immediate followers are in the same frame of mind as their ruler. Since the bombing of Germany *felt good* not only to Roosevelt and Churchill but to the American and British peoples, mere facts, and the desire for a swift victory, could not be allowed to impede the ritual of incineration.

In other words, the leader-led relationship confronts us on a collective scale with the same dilemmas of pretherapeutic "blindness" that we experience in trying to turn the corner on our personal neurotic patterns. The crucially important fact is *always* the one that is most deeply buried, and as we struggle to unblock it we find our psyche flinging into view everything and anything that might distract us from our purpose.

The proper analogy to these intrapsychic defenses against insight is to be sought in the complex symbolisms without which no one can achieve leadership status. During the Depression years, Roosevelt was an exquisitely accurate projection for a nation wallowing in frustration and impotence; during the War, an equally perfect allegory of an angry crippled baby on an exterminatory rampage. But in both periods this projective core was elaborately swaddled, blurred, and denied. The wheelchair could never be photographed, the paralysis could be alluded to only as the prelude to triumph and transcendence, and attention was focused instead on images of Hyde Park, aristocracy, cigarette-holders, stamp collecting, "the famous smile," the splendid partnership with Eleanor, the awesome duties of *noblesse oblige.* Potency, competency, control—rulership eternally unruffled by mundane considerations—were the compensatory and antithetical images with which the perceived truth was denied out of existence.

Since we can barely achieve comparable insight for more recent leaders like John F. Kennedy and Lyndon Johnson—while the gross pathology of Richard Nixon is treated as a personal rather than a collective problem—it seems almost impossible to crack, in an adequate way, the even more immediate puzzle of Jimmy Carter. That this particular individual was chosen to "lead" us seems, after all, just as unlikely as Roosevelt did in 1932, Kennedy in 1960, and Richard Nixon in 1968, before sheer habituation made the weird seem normal and predestined. And what we are trying to do, in effect, is to sort out the elements in a collective fantasy that we tend to reimmerse ourselves in each time we pick up a newspaper or turn on the television—rather as if our therapist had a competitor in the same room whose goal was to terminate our insights and keep us bound in the world of unreality.

The crucial clue in beginning to do this lies, it seems to me, in the saving fact that every denial system contains a hidden acknowledgement of the truth being denied: the primary dialectic without which psychoanalytic insight would be nearly impossible. And where our leaders are concerned, this implies a nearly instantaneous recognition—like a flash-bulb popping—of what he or she is "all about," followed in milliseconds by repression, denial, and the construction, at the individual as well as the collective level, of an inverted "myth." The hypothesis which I am proposing, and for the correctness of which there is a good deal of support in recent history, is that none of us is dumb but that all of us are repression junkies. On this model, there is no Republican, not even one from Arizona or Southern California, who needs Dr. Abrahamsen to tell him a single thing about Richard Nixon. They knew it all along. Repression is called repression—rather than, say, "mild forgetting"—*because* it represents the eradication from consciousness of the most important truths we have ever learned: the truth, for example, that Mama doesn't love us, or that the President is just as nutty as Daddy. And on this model, even David Beisel's admirable study in this set of essays will come as news only to the *consciousness* of its readers, not to mention its (predictably) indignant critics.

If the leader's "myth" is the inversion of how he is perceived at the unconscious level, and if the unconscious perception ultimately determines the role he feels called upon to play—the role that becomes clearer with two or three decades of hindsight—then what kind of baby is Jimmy Carter, and what is he likely to do with us and to us?

My answer to this question is so distressingly crude that I feel some hesitation about committing it to paper. But I will persevere, with the tangential observation that discussion of issues like these makes me nearly as anxious, and therefore reluctant to proceed, as it may be making the reader of this essay.

One of the paradoxes in psychohistorical and psychobiographical analysis of recent presidencies is that this very activity—which has been condemned (most recently by Dr. Peter Bourne) as illegitimate—is taking place within a cultural and historical context that has repeatedly shown a "psychiatric" concern about the candidates for the highest office. Adlai Stevenson was perhaps the first candidate whose defeat could be attributed to the conviction, artfully exploited by his opponents, that he was *psychologically* inadequate for the role of leader. To the doubts publicly entertained in 1964 about the sanity of Barry Goldwater and the withdrawal of Thomas Eagleton can be added the recurrent hints, dating from the 1960's, that Richard Nixon had been seeing a psychiatrist and had deeper problems than anyone suspected. As we have moved ever more deeply into an age of psychology, "popular feeling" has increasingly reflected the notion, or the fear, that the occupant of the White

House might turn out—if we are not extremely vigilant—to be clinically nuts.

The fact that one candidate has been repeatedly scapegoated in this manner, while his opponent is described, overtly or by suggestion, as a triumphantly healthy and competent specimen, suggests to me that the group projections and inherent irrationalities that are the subject of this essay (and of the other essays in this issue) are becoming more accessible to consciousness even among those who have no psychological training or ambitions. If the students of group process are correct, and the leader is in fact the receiver and vehicle for feelings that cannot be "owned" by his constituency, then the governmental processes described with such detachment and tedium in civics courses are in fact as crazy as any hallucinating "schizophrenic." And of course the *true* fear—that the man actually ruling the country is a loony—can be handled only by the reassuring reflection that insanity was eliminated in the person of his opponent.

In turn, the suspicion that the President may be nuts cannot—in view of his entirely projective function—be dissociated from the growing suspicion, by "average" Americans in "average" American families, that *they* may be nuts. We seem to have reached a transitional interpretive moment halfway between the older assumption that "mental illness" is a problem somewhere *out there*—one that reasonable people like you and me are concerned about on charitable grounds—and a full acceptance of the psychopathology of our everyday lives, which includes our relationship to Presidents, Führers, Generalissimos, and Imperators.

In this connection, it seems absolutely crucial (1) that Jimmy Carter is the product of a typically problematic family whose problematic qualities were perceived *before* the election, and (2) that he should be the first President in history to champion, with his wife and one of his closest advisors, a cause called "mental health." In psychotherapeutic circles, the suggestion has circulated that crusading for "mental health," and striking up what amounts to a virtual alliance with the nation's psychologists, is the Carter way of admitting that all is much less than "well" in the Carter family. But the psychotherapists are barely a step ahead of the American layman, whose understanding, as I have already indicated, should not be confused with what he can consciously articulate.

At the unconscious level, in other words, the Carter family, with its bizarre admixture of rednecks, faith-healers, convicts, and puritanical obsessive-compulsives, is perceived as being just as distorted and "crazy" as the families of "average" American voters: a Munster clan or Addams family that has somehow wandered off the TV screen and into the White House. The concern with "mental health," which for the Carters themselves may be a quasi-therapeutic involvement in other people's problems, is politically necessary to counter-balance this image at two suggestive levels. At the more superficial level, it encourages a line of reasoning that sees a concern for "mental health" as precluding the possibility that the one who is concerned is himself or herself ill. At a deeper level lies the suggestion that a healer, if not completely healthy, is still ultimately capable of healing himself, and thereafter of healing us.

The allegorical and projective function of Jimmy Carter and his family, therefore, is to prove that all is not hopeless for us Jukes, Kallikaks, and Munsters, and that we are not as nauseatingly ill as Jerry Rubin, Abbie Hoffman, and Richard Nixon so brilliantly implied. And the evangelical strain in the Carter background, with its emphasis on rebirth and renewal, harmonizes perfectly with this psychotherapeutic quest.

To the extent that the Carters are seen as projective and magical saviors of a sick and sickened commonwealth, our political processes are just as crazy as they ever were. Worse yet, they are setting the stage for an inevitable disappointment that may open the door to behavior at considerable variance with the ideals of Human Rights. There is enough neo-Darwinian thinking in the air right now to make a reversion to warlike and severely repressive ideation at least a possibility, and Carter's military background is an element that must never be omitted from our psychological "montage" of the appeal he makes to the American unconscious. At the same time, we must acknowledge the effort he somehow represents to be much more open, and therefore much healthier, about one's inner life. We the people, between these shores assembled, are a great beast. But the beast is slowly learning that that horror in the mirror belongs to *him*. Baby is trying, in this odd way he has, to get well.

Henry Ebel, Ph.D., is Editor of Behavior Today, *a Research Associate of The Institute for Psychohistory, Associate Editor of* The Journal of Psychohistory, *and the author of several books and articles on psychohistory.*

Index
by Barbara M. Preschel